WHAT'S COOKING

pasta

Tom Bridge

This is a Parragon Book
This edition published in 2000

Parragon
Queen Street House
4 Queen Street
Bath BA1 1HE, UK

ISBN: 0-75253-850-0 (Paperback)
ISBN: 0-75253-856-X (Hardback)

Printed in Indonesia

Produced by Haldane Mason, London

Acknowledgements
Art Director: Ron Samuels
Editorial Director: Sydney Francis
Editorial Consultant: Christopher Fagg
Managing Editor: Jo-Anne Cox
Editor: Linda A. Doeser
Design: Digital Artworks Partnership Ltd
Photography: Andrew Sydenham
Home Economist: Victoria Simister

Note
Cup measurements in this book are for American cups.
Tablespoons are assumed to be 15 ml. Unless otherwise stated,
milk is assumed to be full fat, eggs are medium
and pepper is freshly ground black pepper.

Contents

Introduction

Pasta has existed in one form or another since the days of the Roman Empire and remains one of the most versatile ingredients in the kitchen. It can be combined with almost anything from meat to fish, vegetables to fruit and is even delicious served with simple herb sauces. No store cupboard should be without a supply of dried pasta, which, combined with a few other stock ingredients, can be turned into a mouth-watering and nutritious meal within minutes.

Most pasta is made from durum wheat flour and contains protein and carbohydrates. It is a good source of slow-release energy and has the additional advantage of being value for money.

There is an enormous range of different types of pasta, some of which are listed on the opposite page. Many are available both dried and fresh. Unless you have access to a good, Italian delicatessen, it is probably not worth buying fresh unfilled pasta, but even supermarkets sell high-quality tortellini, capelletti, ravioli and agnolotti.

Best of all, is to make fresh pasta at home. It takes a little time, but is quite easy and well worth the effort. You can mix the dough by hand or prepare it in a food processor.

Pasta may be coloured and flavoured with extra ingredients that are usually added with the beaten egg:

Black: add 1 tsp squid or cuttlefish ink.
Green: add 115 g/4 oz well-drained, cooked spinach when kneading.
Purple: work 1 large, cooked beetroot (beet) in a food processor and add with an extra 60 g/2 oz/½ cup flour.
Red: add 2 tbsp tomato purée (paste).

Always use a large saucepan for cooking pasta and bring lightly salted water to the boil. Add the pasta and 1 tbsp olive oil, but do not cover or the water will boil over. Quickly bring the water back to a rolling boil and avoid overcooking. When the pasta is tender, but still firm to the bite, drain and toss with butter, olive oil or your prepared sauce and serve as soon as possible.

The cooking times given here are guidelines only:

Fresh unfilled pasta: *2–3 minutes*
Fresh filled pasta: *8–10 minutes*
Dried unfilled pasta: *10–12 minutes*
Dried filled pasta: *15–20 minutes*

BASIC PASTA DOUGH

If you wish to make your own pasta for the dishes in this book, follow this simple recipe.

Serves 4

INGREDIENTS
450 g/1 lb/4 cups durum wheat flour
4 eggs, lightly beaten
1 tbsp olive oil
salt

1 Lightly flour a work surface (counter). Sift the flour with a pinch of salt into a mound. Make a well in the centre and add the eggs and olive oil.

2 Using a fork or your fingertips, gradually work the mixture until the ingredients are combined. Knead vigorously for 10–15 minutes.

3 Set the dough aside to rest for 25 minutes, before rolling it out as thinly and evenly as possible.

TYPES OF PASTA

There are as many as 200 different pasta shapes and about three times as many names for them. New shapes are being designed – and named – all the time and the same shape may be called a different name in different regions of Italy.

anelli, anellini: *small rings for soup*

bucatini: *long, medium-thick tubes*

cannelloni: *large, thick, round pasta tubes*

capelli d'angelo: *thin strands of 'angel hair'*

conchiglie: *ridged shells*

conchigliette: *little shells*

cresti di gallo: *curved-shaped*

ditali, ditalini: *short tubes*

eliche: *loose spirals*

farfalle: *bows*

fettuccine: *medium ribbons*

fusilli: *spirals*

gemelli: *two pieces wrapped together as 'twins'*

lasagne: *flat, rectangular sheets*

linguini: *long, flat ribbons*

lumache: *snail-shaped shells*

lumaconi: *big shells*

macaroni: *long- or short-cut tubes*

orecchiette: *ear-shaped*

penne: *quill-shaped*

rigatoni: *thick, ridged tubes*

spaghetti: *fine or medium rods*

tagliarini: *thin ribbons*

tagliatelle: *broad ribbons*

vermicelli: *fine pasta, usually folded into skeins*

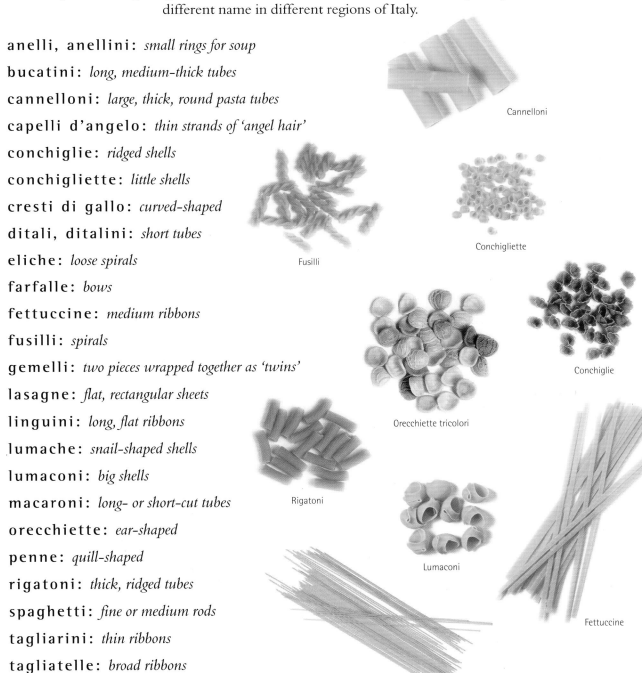

Cannelloni

Fusilli

Conchigliette

Conchiglie

Orecchiette tricolori

Rigatoni

Lumaconi

Fettuccine

Spaghetti

Soups & Light Meals

Pasta is so versatile: it can be used to make soups more substantial, as a delicious and unusual starter or as a quick and easy lunch or light supper. The recipes in this chapter range from traditional Italian dishes, such as Minestrone soup and Spaghetti alla Carbonara, to intriguing new ways with pasta, such as Pancetta & Pecorino Cakes with Farfalle and Pasta Omelette.

Soup recipes include filling winter dishes that, if served with some crusty bread, make a meal in themselves. Try Haricot Bean & Pasta Soup, for example. Others, like Cream of Lemon & Chicken Soup, are subtle and delicate. Recipes for snacks and light meals offer something for every taste – vegetable, cheese, meat and fish sauces combined with every pasta shape from linguine to lumache. Try Smoked Ham Linguine if you are in a hurry, or Creamed Veal Kidneys with Penne if you want something a little different.

Minestrone

*Italian cooks have created some very heart-warming
soups and this is the most famous of all.*

Serves 8–10

INGREDIENTS

3 garlic cloves
3 large onions
2 celery sticks (sticks)
2 large carrots
2 large potatoes
100 g/3^1/2 oz French (green) beans
100 g/3^1/2 oz courgettes (zucchini)

60 g/2 oz/4 tbsp butter
50 ml/2 fl oz/^{1}/4 cup olive oil
60 g/2 oz rindless fatty bacon,
   finely diced
1.5 litres/2^3/4 pints/6^7/8 cups
   vegetable or chicken stock
1 bunch fresh basil, finely chopped

100 g/3^1/2 oz chopped tomatoes
2 tbsp tomato purée (paste)
100 g/3^1/2 oz Parmesan cheese rind
85 g/3 oz dried spaghetti, broken up
salt and pepper
freshly grated Parmesan cheese,
   to serve

1 Finely chop the garlic, onions,
celery, carrots, potatoes, beans
and courgettes (zucchini).

2 Heat the butter and oil
together in a large saucepan,
add the bacon and cook for 2
minutes. Add the garlic and onion
and fry for 2 minutes, then stir in
the celery, carrots and potatoes
and fry for a further 2 minutes.

3 Add the beans to the pan and
fry for 2 minutes. Stir in the

courgettes (zucchini) and fry for
a further 2 minutes. Cover the pan
and cook all the vegetables, stirring
frequently, for 15 minutes.

4 Add the stock, basil, tomatoes,
tomato purée (paste) and
cheese rind and season to taste.
Bring to the boil, lower the heat
and simmer for 1 hour. Remove
and discard the cheese rind.

5 Add the spaghetti to the pan
and cook for 20 minutes.

Serve in large, warm soup bowls
sprinkled with freshly grated
Parmesan cheese.

COOK'S TIP

*There are almost as
many recipes for
minestrone as there
are cooks in Italy!*
*You can add almost any vegetables
you like, including soaked
dried beans.*

Italian Cream of Tomato Soup

*Plum tomatoes are ideal for making soups and sauces, as
they have denser, less watery flesh than round varieties.*

Serves 4

INGREDIENTS

60 g/2 oz/4 tbsp unsalted butter
1 large onion, chopped
600 ml/1 pint/2¹⁄₂ cups
   vegetable stock
900 g/2 lb Italian plum tomatoes,
   skinned and roughly chopped

pinch of bicarbonate of soda
   (baking soda)
225 g/8 oz/2 cups dried fusilli
1 tbsp caster (superfine) sugar
150 ml/¹⁄₄ pint/⁵⁄₈ cup double
   (heavy) cream

salt and pepper
fresh basil leaves, to garnish
deep-fried croûtons, to serve

1 Melt the butter in a large pan, add the onion and fry for 3 minutes. Add 300 ml/½ pint/1¼ cups of vegetable stock to the pan, with the chopped tomatoes and bicarbonate of soda (baking soda). Bring the soup to the boil and simmer for 20 minutes.

2 Remove the pan from the heat and set aside to cool. Purée the soup in a blender or food processor and pour through a fine strainer back into the saucepan.

3 Add the remaining vegetable stock and the fusilli to the pan, and season to taste with salt and pepper.

4 Add the sugar to the pan, bring to the boil, then lower the heat and simmer for about 15 minutes.

5 Pour the soup into a warm tureen, swirl the double (heavy) cream around the surface of the soup and garnish with fresh basil leaves. Serve immediately.

VARIATION

To make orange and tomato soup, simply use half the quantity of vegetable stock, topped up with the same amount of fresh orange juice and garnish the soup with orange rind. Or to make tomato and carrot soup, add half the quantity again of vegetable stock with the same amount of carrot juice and 175 g/6 oz/1¼ cups grated carrot to the recipe, cooking the carrot with the onion.

Potato & Parsley Soup with Pesto

Fresh pesto is a treat to the taste buds and very different in flavour from the jars of pesto available from supermarkets.

Serves 4

INGREDIENTS

3 slices rindless, smoked, fatty bacon
25 g/1 oz/2 tbsp butter
450 g/1 lb floury potatoes
450 g/ 1 lb onions
600 ml/1 pint/2^1/2 cups chicken stock
600 ml/1 pint/2^1/2 cups milk
100 g/3^1/2 oz/^{3}/4 cup
  dried conchigliette
150 ml/^{1}/4 pint/^{5}/8 cup double
  (heavy) cream

chopped fresh parsley
salt and black pepper
freshly grated Parmesan cheese and
  garlic bread, to serve

PESTO SAUCE:
60 g/2 oz/1 cup finely chopped
  fresh parsley
2 garlic cloves, crushed

60 g/2 oz/^{2}/3 cup pine nuts
  (kernels), crushed
2 tbsp chopped fresh basil leaves
60 g/2 oz/^{2}/3 cup freshly grated
  Parmesan cheese
white pepper
150 ml/^{1}/4 pint/^{5}/8 cup olive oil

1 To make the pesto sauce, put all of the ingredients in a blender or food processor and process for 2 minutes, or blend together by hand (see Cook's Tip).

2 Finely chop the bacon, potatoes and onions. Fry the bacon in a large pan over a medium heat for 4 minutes. Add the butter, potatoes and onions and cook for 12 minutes, stirring constantly.

3 Add the stock and milk to the pan, bring to the boil and simmer for 10 minutes. Add the conchigliette and simmer for a further 12-14 minutes.

4 Blend in the cream and simmer for 5 minutes. Add the parsley and 2 tbsp pesto sauce. Transfer the soup to serving bowls and serve with Parmesan cheese and fresh garlic bread.

COOK'S TIP

If you are making pesto by hand, it is best to use a mortar and pestle. Thoroughly grind together the parsley, garlic, pine nuts (kernels) and basil to make a paste, then mix in the cheese and pepper. Finally, gradually beat in the oil.

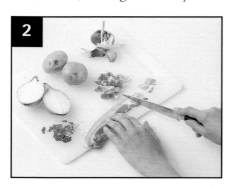

Ravioli alla Parmigiana

This soup is the traditional 'Minestra' served at Easter and Christmas in the province of Parma.

Serves 4

INGREDIENTS

285 g/10 oz Basic Pasta Dough
    (see page 4)
1.2 litres/2 pints/5 cups veal stock
freshly grated Parmesan cheese,
    to serve

FILLING:
100 g/3¹/₂ oz/1 cup freshly grated
    Parmesan cheese
100 g/3¹/₂ oz/1²/₃ cup fine
    white breadcrumbs
2 eggs

125 ml/4 fl oz/¹/₂ cup Espagnole
    Sauce (see Cook's Tip, below)
1 small onion, finely chopped
1 tsp freshly grated nutmeg

1 Make the basic pasta dough (see page 4). Carefully roll out 2 sheets of the pasta dough and cover with a damp tea towel (dish cloth) while you make the filling for the ravioli.

2 To make the filling, mix together the freshly grated Parmesan cheese, fine white breadcrumbs, eggs, espagnole sauce (see Cook's Tip, right), finely chopped onion and the freshly grated nutmeg in a large mixing bowl.

3 Place spoonfuls of the filling at regular intervals on 1 sheet of pasta dough. Cover with the second sheet of pasta dough, then cut into squares and seal the edges.

4 Bring the veal stock to the boil in a large saucepan. Add the ravioli to the pan and cook for about 15 minutes.

5 Transfer the soup and ravioli to warm serving bowls and serve at once, generously sprinkled with Parmesan cheese.

COOK'S TIP

For espagnole sauce, melt 2 tbsp butter and stir in 25 g/1 oz/¼ cup plain flour. Cook over a low heat, stirring, until lightly coloured. Add 1 tsp tomato purée (paste), then stir in 250 ml/9 fl oz/1⅛ cups hot veal stock, 1 tbsp Madeira and 1½ tsp white wine vinegar. Dice 25 g/1 oz each bacon, carrot and onion and 15 g/½ oz each celery, leek and fennel. Fry with a thyme sprig and a bay leaf in oil until soft. Drain, add to the sauce and simmer for 4 hours. Strain before using.

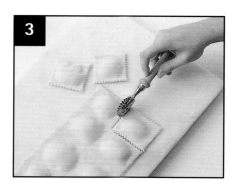

Pea & Egg Noodle Soup with Parmesan Cheese Croûtons

This is a delicious and filling treat on cold winter evenings.

Serves 4

INGREDIENTS

3 slices smoked, rindless fatty
  bacon, diced
1 large onion, chopped
15 g/$^1/_2$ oz/1 tbsp butter

450 g/1 lb/2$^1/_2$ cups dried peas,
  soaked in cold water for 2 hours
  and drained
2.3 litres/4 pints/10 cups
  chicken stock
225 g/ 8 oz dried egg noodles

150 ml/$^1/_4$ pint/$^5/_8$ cup double
  (heavy) cream
salt and pepper
chopped fresh parsley, to garnish
Parmesan cheese croûtons (see
  Cook's Tip, below), to serve

1 Put the bacon, onion and butter into a large saucepan and cook over a low heat for about 6 minutes.

2 Add the peas and the chicken stock to the pan and bring to the boil. Season lightly with salt and pepper, cover and simmer for 1½ hours.

3 Add the egg noodles to the pan and simmer for a further 15 minutes.

4 Pour in the cream and blend thoroughly. Transfer to a warm tureen, garnish with parsley and top with Parmesan cheese croûtons (see Cook's Tip, right). Serve immediately.

VARIATION

Other pulses, such as dried haricot (navy) beans, borlotti or pinto beans, may be substituted for the peas in this recipe.

COOK'S TIP

To make Parmesan cheese croûtons, cut a French stick into slices. Coat each slice lightly with olive oil and sprinkle with Parmesan cheese. Grill (broil) for about 30 seconds.

Haricot (Navy) Bean & Pasta Soup

This soup makes an excellent winter lunch served with
warm crusty bread and a slice of cheese.

Serves 4

INGREDIENTS

250 g/9 oz/1^1/$_3$ cups haricot (navy)
   beans, soaked for 3 hours in cold
   water and drained
4 tbsp olive oil
2 large onions, sliced
3 garlic cloves, chopped
425 g/14 oz can chopped tomatoes

1 tsp dried oregano
1 tsp tomato purée (paste)
850 ml/1^1/$_2$ pints/3^1/$_2$ cups water
90 g/3^1/$_2$ oz/^{3}/$_4$ cup dried fusilli
   or conchigliette
115 g/4 oz sun-dried tomatoes,
   drained and thinly sliced

1 tbsp chopped fresh coriander
   (cilantro) or flat leaf parsley
salt and pepper
2 tbsp Parmesan cheese shavings,
   to serve

1 Put the haricot (navy) beans in a large saucepan, add sufficient cold water to cover and bring to the boil. Boil vigorously over a high heat for 15 minutes. Drain and keep warm.

2 Heat the oil in a pan over medium heat and fry the onions for 2–3 minutes or until they are just beginning to change colour. Stir in the garlic and cook for 1 minute. Stir in the tomatoes, oregano and tomato purée (paste).

3 Add the water and the reserved beans to the pan. Bring to the boil, cover, then lower the heat and simmer for about 45 minutes, or until the beans are almost tender.

4 Add the pasta to the pan and season to taste with salt and pepper. Stir in the sun-dried tomatoes, bring back to the boil, partly cover and simmer for 10 minutes, or until the pasta is tender, but still firm to the bite.

5 Stir the coriander (cilantro) or parsley into the soup. Ladle the soup into a warm tureen, sprinkle over the Parmesan cheese and serve immediately.

COOK'S TIP

If preferred, place the beans in a pan of cold water and bring to the boil. Remove from the heat and leave the beans to cool in the water. Drain and rinse before using.

Chick Pea (Garbanzo Bean) & Chicken Soup

This hearty and nourishing soup is an ideal starter for a family supper.

Serves 4

INGREDIENTS

25 g/1 oz/2 tbsp butter
3 spring onions (scallions), chopped
2 garlic cloves, crushed
1 fresh marjoram sprig,
  finely chopped
350 g/12 oz boned chicken
  breasts, diced

350 g/12 oz can chick peas
  (garbanzo beans), drained
1.2 litres/2 pints/5 cups chicken stock
1 bouquet garni
1 red (bell) pepper, diced
1 green (bell) pepper, diced

115 g/4 oz/1 cup small dried pasta
  shapes, such as elbow macaroni
salt and white pepper
croûtons, to serve

1 Melt the butter in a large saucepan. Add the spring onions (scallions), garlic, sprig of fresh marjoram and the diced chicken and cook, stirring frequently, over a medium heat for 5 minutes.

2 Add the chicken stock, chick peas (garbanzo beans) and bouquet garni to the pan and season to taste with salt and white pepper.

3 Bring the soup to the boil, lower the heat and then simmer gently for about 2 hours.

4 Add the diced (bell) peppers and pasta to the pan, then simmer for a further 20 minutes.

5 Transfer the soup to a warm tureen. To serve, ladle the soup into individual serving bowls and serve immediately garnished with the croûtons.

COOK'S TIP

If you prefer, you can use dried chick peas (garbanzo beans). Cover with cold water and set aside to soak for 5–8 hours. Drain and add the beans to the soup, according to the recipe, and allow an additional 30 minutes–1 hour cooking time.

Cream of Lemon & Chicken Soup with Spaghetti

This delicately flavoured summer soup is surprisingly easy to make.

Serves 4

INGREDIENTS

60 g/2 oz/4 tbsp butter
8 shallots, thinly sliced
2 carrots, thinly sliced
2 celery sticks (stalks), thinly sliced
225 g/8 oz boned chicken breasts,
   finely chopped

3 lemons
1.2 litres/2 pints/5 cups chicken stock
225 g/8 oz dried spaghetti, broken
   into small pieces
150 ml/$\frac{1}{4}$ pint/$\frac{5}{8}$ cup double
   (heavy) cream

salt and white pepper

TO GARNISH:
fresh parsley sprig
3 lemon slices, halved

1 Melt the butter in a large saucepan. Add the shallots, carrots, celery and chicken and cook over a low heat, stirring occasionally, for 8 minutes.

2 Thinly pare the lemons and blanch the lemon rind in boiling water for 3 minutes. Squeeze the juice from the lemons.

3 Add the lemon rind and juice to the pan, together with the chicken stock. Bring slowly to the boil over a low heat and simmer for 40 minutes.

4 Add the spaghetti to the pan and cook for 15 minutes. Season to taste with salt and white pepper and add the cream. Heat through, but do not allow the soup to boil or it will curdle.

5 Pour the soup into a tureen or individual bowls, garnish with the parsley and half slices of lemon and serve immediately.

COOK'S TIP

You can prepare this soup up to the end of step 3 in advance, so that all you need do before serving is heat it through before adding the pasta and the finishing touches.

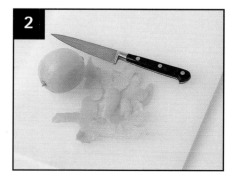

Chicken & Sweetcorn Soup

This heart-warming soup is both quick and easy to make.

Serves 4

INGREDIENTS

450 g/1 lb boned chicken breasts, cut into strips
1.2 litres/2 pints/5 cups chicken stock
150 ml/^{1}/4 pint/^{5}/8 cup double (heavy) cream

100 g/3^1/2 oz/^{3}/4 cup dried vermicelli
1 tbsp cornflour (cornstarch)
3 tbsp milk

175 g/6 oz sweetcorn (corn-on-the-cob) kernels
salt and pepper

1 Put the chicken, stock and cream into a large saucepan and bring to the boil over a low heat. Reduce the heat slightly and simmer for about 20 minutes. Season the soup with salt and black pepper to taste.

2 Meanwhile, cook the vermicelli in lightly salted boiling water for 10-12 minutes, until just tender. Drain the pasta and keep warm.

3 In a small bowl, mix together the cornflour (cornstarch) and milk to make a smooth paste.

Stir the cornflour (cornstarch) into the soup until thickened.

4 Add the sweetcorn (corn-on-the-cob) and vermicelli to the pan and heat through.

5 Transfer the soup to a warm tureen or individual soup bowls and serve immediately.

COOK'S TIP

If you are short of time, buy ready-cooked chicken, remove any skin and cut it into slices.

VARIATION

For crab and sweetcorn soup, substitute 450 g/1 lb cooked crabmeat for the chicken breasts. Flake the crabmeat well before adding it to the saucepan and reduce the cooking time by 10 minutes. For a Chinese-style soup, substitute egg noodles for the vermicelli and use canned, creamed sweetcorn (corn-on-the-cob).

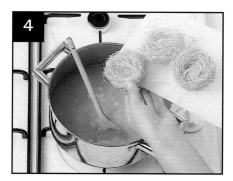

Veal & Ham Soup with Sherry

Veal and ham is a classic combination, used here to good effect to create a richly-flavoured Italian soup.

Serves 4

INGREDIENTS

60 g/2 oz/4 tbsp butter
1 onion, diced
1 carrot, diced
1 celery stick (stalk), diced
450 g/1 lb very thinly sliced veal
450 g/1 lb thinly sliced ham

60 g/2 oz/^{1}/$_2$ cup plain
  (all purpose) flour
1 litre/1^3/$_4$ pints/4^3/$_8$ cups beef stock
1 bay leaf
8 black peppercorns
pinch of salt

3 tbsp redcurrant jelly
150 ml/^{1}/$_4$ pint/^{5}/$_8$ cup cream sherry
100 g/3^1/$_2$ oz/^{3}/$_4$ cup dried vermicelli
garlic croûtons, to serve

1 Melt the butter in a large saucepan. Add the onions, carrot, celery, veal and ham and cook over a low heat for about 6 minutes.

2 Sprinkle over the flour and cook, stirring constantly, for a further 2 minutes. Gradually stir in the stock, then add the bay leaf, peppercorns and salt. Bring to the boil and simmer for 1 hour.

3 Remove the pan from the heat and add the redcurrant jelly and cream sherry. Set aside for about 4 hours.

4 Remove the bay leaf from the pan and discard. Reheat the soup over a very low heat until warmed through.

5 Meanwhile, cook the vermicelli in a saucepan of lightly salted boiling water for 10-12 minutes. Stir the vermicelli into the soup and transfer to warm soup bowls. Serve with garlic croûtons (see Cook's Tip, right).

COOK'S TIP

To make garlic croûtons, remove the crusts from 3 slices of day-old white bread. Cut the bread into 5 mm/ ¼ inch cubes. Heat 3 tbsp olive oil over a low heat and stir-fry 1–2 finely chopped garlic cloves for 1–2 minutes. Remove the garlic and add the bread. Cook, tossing the pan and stirring frequently, until golden brown. Remove from the pan with a slotted spoon and drain on kitchen paper (towels).

Tuscan Veal Broth

Veal plays an important role in Italian cuisine and there are dozens of recipes for all cuts of this meat.

Serves 4

INGREDIENTS

60 g/2 oz/^{1}/$_3$ cup dried peas, soaked
   for 2 hours and drained
900 g/2 lb boned neck of
   veal, diced
1.2 litres/2 pints/5 cups beef or
   brown stock (see Cook's Tip)

600 ml/1 pint/2^1/$_2$ cups water
60 g/2 oz/^{1}/$_3$ cup barley, washed
1 large carrot, diced
1 small turnip (about 175 g/6 oz),
   diced
1 large leek, thinly sliced

1 red onion, finely chopped
100 g/3^1/$_2$ oz chopped tomatoes
1 fresh basil sprig
100 g/3^1/$_2$ oz/^{3}/$_4$ cup dried vermicelli
salt and white pepper

1 Put the peas, veal, stock and water into a large saucepan and bring to the boil over a low heat. Using a slotted spoon, skim off any scum that rises to the surface of the liquid.

2 When all of the scum has been removed, add the barley and a pinch of salt to the mixture. Simmer gently over a low heat for 25 minutes.

3 Add the carrot, turnip, leek, onion, tomatoes and basil to the pan, and season with salt and pepper to taste. Leave to simmer for about 2 hours, skimming the surface, using a slotted spoon, from time to time. Remove the pan from the heat and set aside for 2 hours.

4 Set the pan over a medium heat and bring to the boil. Add the vermicelli and cook for 12 minutes. Season with salt and pepper to taste and remove and discard the basil. Ladle into soup bowls and serve immediately.

COOK'S TIP

The best brown stock is made with veal bones and shin of beef roasted with dripping (drippings) in the oven for 40 minutes. Transfer the bones to a large pan and add sliced leeks, onion, celery and carrots, a bouquet garni, white wine vinegar and a thyme sprig and cover with cold water. Simmer over a very low heat for about 3 hours. Strain and blot the fat from the surface with kitchen paper (towels).

Veal & Wild Mushroom Soup with Vermicelli

Wild mushrooms are available commercially and an increasing range of cultivated varieties is now to be found in many supermarkets.

Serves 4

INGREDIENTS

450 g/1 lb veal, thinly sliced
450 g/1 lb veal bones
1.2 litres/2 pints/5 cups water
1 small onion
6 peppercorns
1 tsp cloves

pinch of mace
140 g/5 oz oyster and shiitake
　mushrooms, roughly chopped
150 ml/^{1}/$_4$ pint/^{5}/$_8$ cup double
　(heavy) cream

100 g/3^1/$_2$ oz/^{3}/$_4$ cup dried vermicelli
1 tbsp cornflour (cornstarch)
3 tbsp milk
salt and pepper

1 Put the veal, bones and water into a large saucepan. Bring to the boil and lower the heat. Add the onion, peppercorns, cloves and mace and simmer for about 3 hours, until the veal stock is reduced by one-third.

2 Strain the stock, skim off any fat on the surface with a slotted spoon, and pour the stock into a clean saucepan. Add the veal meat to the pan.

3 Add the mushrooms and cream, bring to the boil over a low heat and simmer for 12 minutes. Meanwhile, cook the vermicelli in lightly salted boiling water until tender, but still firm to the bite. Drain and keep warm.

4 Mix together the cornflour (cornstarch) and milk to form a smooth paste. Stir into the soup to thicken. Season to taste with salt and pepper and just before serving, add the vermicelli. Transfer the soup to a warm tureen and serve immediately.

COOK'S TIP

You can make this soup with the more inexpensive cuts of veal, such as breast or neck slices. These are lean and the long cooking time ensures that the meat is really tender.

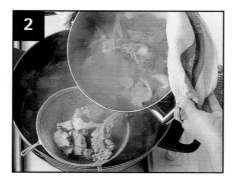

Mussel & Potato Soup

This quick and easy soup would make a delicious
summer lunch served with fresh crusty bread.

Serves 4

INGREDIENTS

750 g/1 lb 10 oz mussels
2 tbsp olive oil
100 g/3$^{1}/_{2}$ oz/7 tbsp unsalted butter
2 slices rindless fatty bacon, chopped
1 onion, chopped
2 garlic cloves, crushed

60 g/2 oz/$^{1}/_{2}$ cup plain
 (all purpose) flour
450 g/1 lb potatoes, thinly sliced
100 g/3$^{1}/_{2}$ oz/$^{3}/_{4}$ cup
 dried conchigliette
300 ml/$^{1}/_{2}$ pint/1$^{1}/_{4}$ cups double
 (heavy) cream

1 tbsp lemon juice
2 egg yolks
salt and pepper

TO GARNISH:
2 tbsp finely chopped fresh parsley
lemon wedges

1 Debeard the mussels and scrub them under cold water for 5 minutes. Discard any mussels that do not close immediately when sharply tapped.

2 Bring a large pan of water to the boil, add the mussels, oil and a little pepper and cook until the mussels open.

3 Drain the mussels, reserving the cooking liquid. Discard any mussels that are closed. Remove the mussels from their shells.

4 Melt the butter in a large saucepan, add the bacon, onion and garlic and cook for 4 minutes. Carefully stir in the flour. Measure 1.2 litres/2 pints/ 5 cups of the reserved cooking liquid and stir it into the pan.

5 Add the potatoes to the pan and simmer for 5 minutes. Add the conchigliette and simmer for a further 10 minutes.

6 Add the cream and lemon juice, season to taste with salt

and pepper, then add the mussels to the pan.

7 Blend the egg yolks with 1-2 tbsp of the remaining cooking liquid, stir into the pan and cook for 4 minutes.

8 Ladle the soup into 4 warm individual soup bowls, garnish with the chopped fresh parsley and lemon wedges and serve immediately.

Italian Fish Soup

This colourful mixed seafood soup would be
superbly complemented by a dry white wine.

Serves 4

INGREDIENTS

60 g/2 oz/4 tbsp butter
450 g/1 lb assorted fish fillets, such
   as red mullet and snapper
450 g/1 lb prepared seafood, such as
   squid and prawns (shrimp)
225 g/8 oz fresh crabmeat
1 large onion, sliced

25 g/1 oz/$^1/_4$ cup plain
   (all purpose) flour
1.2 litres/2 pints/5 cups fish stock
100 g/3$^1/_2$ oz/$^3/_4$ cup dried pasta
   shapes, such as ditalini
   or elbow macaroni
1 tbsp anchovy essence

grated rind and juice of 1 orange
50 ml/2 fl oz/$^1/_4$ cup dry sherry
300 ml/$^1/_2$ pint/1$^1/_4$ cups double
   (heavy) cream
salt and black pepper
crusty brown bread, to serve

1 Melt the butter in a large
saucepan, add the fish fillets,
seafood, crabmeat and onion and
cook gently over a low heat for
6 minutes.

2 Add the flour to the mixture,
stirring thoroughly to avoid
any lumps.

3 Gradually add the fish stock,
stirring constantly, until the
soup comes to the boil. Reduce the
heat and simmer for 30 minutes.

4 Add the pasta to the pan and
cook for a further 10 minutes.

5 Stir in the anchovy essence,
orange rind, orange juice,
sherry and double (heavy) cream.
Season to taste with salt and
pepper.

6 Heat the soup until
completely warmed through.
Transfer the soup to a tureen or to
warm soup bowls and serve with
crusty brown bread.

COOK'S TIP

The heads, tails, trimmings and
bones of virtually any non-oily fish
can be used to make fish stock.
Simmer 900 g/2 lb fish pieces in a
large saucepan with 150 ml/5 fl oz
white wine, 1 chopped onion, 1
sliced carrot, 1 sliced celery stick
(stalk), 4 black peppercorns, 1
bouquet garni and 1.75 litres/
3 pints/7½ cups water for
30 minutes, then strain.

Spaghetti alla Carbonara

Ensure that all of the cooked ingredients are as hot as possible before adding the eggs, so that they cook on contact.

Serves 4

INGREDIENTS

425 g/15 oz dried spaghetti
2 tbsp olive oil
1 large onion, thinly sliced
2 garlic cloves, chopped
175 g/6 oz rindless bacon, cut into
  thin strips

25 g/1 oz/2 tbsp butter
175 g/6 oz mushrooms, thinly sliced
300 ml/¹/₂ pint/1¹/₄ cups double
  (heavy) cream
3 eggs, beaten

100 g /3¹/₂ oz/1 cup freshly grated
  Parmesan cheese, plus extra to
  serve (optional)
salt and pepper
fresh sage sprigs, to garnish

1 Warm a large serving dish or bowl. Bring a large pan of lightly salted water to the boil. Add the spaghetti and 1 tbsp of the oil and cook until tender, but still firm to the bite. Drain, return to the pan and keep warm.

2 Meanwhile, heat the remaining oil in a frying pan (skillet) over a medium heat. Add the onion and fry until it is transparent. Add the garlic and bacon and fry until the bacon is crisp. Transfer to the warm plate.

3 Melt the butter in the frying pan (skillet). Add the mushrooms and fry, stirring occasionally, for 3-4 minutes. Return the bacon mixture to the pan. Cover and keep warm.

4 Mix together the cream, eggs and cheese in a large bowl and then season to taste with salt and pepper.

5 Working very quickly, tip the spaghetti into the bacon and mushroom mixture and pour over the eggs. Toss the spaghetti quickly into the egg and cream mixture, using 2 forks, and serve immediately. If you wish, serve with extra grated Parmesan cheese.

COOK'S TIP

The key to success with this recipe is not to overcook the egg. That is why it is important to keep all the ingredients hot enough just to cook the egg and to work rapidly to avoid scrambling it.

Smoked Ham Linguini

Served with freshly made Italian bread or tossed with pesto, this makes a mouth-watering light lunch.

Serves 4

INGREDIENTS

450 g/1 lb dried linguini
450 g/1 lb green broccoli
    florets (flowerets)

225g/8 oz Italian smoked ham
150 ml/¹/₄ pint/⁵/₈ cup Italian Cheese
    Sauce (see Cook's Tip, below right)

salt and pepper
Italian bread, to serve

1 Bring a large pan of lightly salted water to the boil. Add the linguini and broccoli florets and cook for 10 minutes, until the linguini is tender, but still firm to the bite.

2 Drain the linguini and broccoli thoroughly, set aside and keep warm.

3 Meanwhile, make the Italian Cheese Sauce (see Cook's Tip, right).

4 Cut the Italian smoked ham into thin strips. Toss the linguini, broccoli and ham into the Italian Cheese Sauce and gently warm through over a very low heat.

5 Transfer the pasta mixture to a warm serving dish. Sprinkle with black pepper and serve with Italian bread.

COOK'S TIP

There are many types of Italian bread which would be suitable to serve with this dish. Ciabatta is made with olive oil and is available plain and with different ingredients, such as olives or sun-dried tomatoes.

COOK'S TIP

For Italian Cheese Sauce, melt 2 tbsp butter in a pan and stir in 25 g/1/ oz/¹/₄ cup plain (all purpose) flour. Cook, stirring, over a low heat until the roux is light in colour and crumbly in texture.
Stir in 300 ml/¹/₂ pint/1¹/₄ cups hot milk. Cook, stirring, for 15 minutes until thick and smooth. Add a pinch of nutmeg, a pinch of dried thyme, 2 tbsp white wine vinegar and season. Stir in 3 tbsp double (heavy) cream and mix.
Stir in 60 g/2 oz/¹/₂ cup grated Mozzarella cheese, 60 g/2 oz/²/₃ cup grated Parmesan cheese, 1 tsp English mustard and 2 tbsp soured cream.

Chorizo & Wild Mushrooms with a Spicy Vermicelli

Simple and quick to make, this spicy dish will set the taste buds tingling.

Serves 6

INGREDIENTS

680 g/1¹/₂ lb dried vermicelli
125 ml/4 fl oz/¹/₂ cup olive oil
2 garlic cloves
125 g/4¹/₂ oz chorizo, sliced

225 g/8 oz wild mushrooms
3 fresh red chillies, chopped
2 tbsp freshly grated
 Parmesan cheese

salt and pepper
10 anchovy fillets, to garnish

1 Bring a large saucepan of lightly salted water to the boil. Add the vermicelli and 1 tbsp of the oil and cook until just tender, but still firm to the bite. Drain, place on a large, warm serving plate and keep warm.

2 Meanwhile heat the remaining oil in a large frying pan (skillet). Add the garlic and fry for 1 minute. Add the chorizo and wild mushrooms and cook for 4 minutes, then add the chopped chillies and cook for 1 further minute.

3 Pour the chorizo and wild mushroom mixture over the vermicelli and season with a little salt and pepper. Sprinkle over freshly grated Parmesan cheese, garnish with a lattice of anchovy fillets and serve immediately.

VARIATION

Fresh sardines may be used in this recipe in place of the anchovies. However, ensure that you gut and clean the sardines, removing the backbone, before using them.

COOK'S TIP

Always obtain wild mushrooms from a reliable source and never pick them yourself unless you are absolutely certain of their identity. Many varieties of mushrooms are now cultivated and most are virtually indistinguishable from the wild varieties. Mixed colour oyster mushrooms have been used here, but you could also use chanterelles. However, remember that chanterelles tend to shrink during cooking, so you may need more.

Pancetta & Pecorino Cakes on a Bed of Farfalle

This makes an excellent starter served with a topping of pesto or anchovy sauce.

Serves 4

INGREDIENTS

25 g/1 oz/2 tbsp butter, plus extra
 for greasing
100 g/3¹/₂ oz pancetta, rind removed
225 g/8 oz/2 cups self-raising
 (self-rising) flour
75 g/2³/₄ oz/⁷/₈ cup grated
 pecorino cheese

150 ml/¹/₄ pint/⁵/₈ cup milk, plus
 extra for glazing
1 tbsp tomato ketchup
1 tsp Worcestershire sauce
400 g/14 oz/3¹/₂ cups dried farfalle
1 tbsp olive oil
salt and black pepper

3 tbsp Pesto (see page 12) or
 anchovy sauce (optional)
green salad, to serve

1 Grease a baking (cookie) sheet with butter. Grill (broil) the pancetta until it is cooked. Allow the pancetta to cool, then chop finely

2 Sift together the flour and a pinch of salt into a mixing bowl. Add the butter and rub in with your fingertips. When the butter and flour have been thoroughly incorporated, add the pancetta and one-third of the grated cheese.

3 Mix together the milk, tomato ketchup and Worcestershire sauce and add to the dry ingredients, mixing to make a soft dough.

4 Roll out the dough on a lightly floured board to make an 18 cm/7 inch round. Brush with a little milk to glaze and cut into 8 wedges.

5 Arrange the dough wedges on the prepared baking (cookie)

sheet and sprinkle over the remaining cheese. Bake in a preheated oven at 200°C/400°F/ Gas 6 for 20 minutes.

6 Meanwhile, bring a saucepan of lightly salted water to the boil. Add the farfalle and the oil and cook until just tender, but still firm to the bite. Drain and transfer to a large serving dish. Top with the pancetta and pecorino cakes. Serve with the sauce of your choice and a green salad.

Orecchiette with Bacon & Tomatoes

*As this dish cooks, the mouth-watering aroma of
bacon, sweet tomatoes and oregano is a feast in itself.*

Serves 4

INGREDIENTS

900 g/2 lb small, sweet tomatoes
6 slices rindless smoked bacon
60 g/2 oz/4 tbsp butter
1 onion, chopped

1 garlic clove, crushed
4 fresh oregano sprigs,
 finely chopped
450 g/1 lb/4 cups dried orecchiette

1 tbsp olive oil
salt and pepper
freshly grated Pecorino cheese,
 to serve

1 Blanch the tomatoes in boiling water. Drain, skin and seed the tomatoes, then roughly chop the flesh. Chop the bacon into small dice.

2 Melt the butter in a saucepan. Add the bacon and fry until it is golden. Add the onion and garlic and fry over a medium heat for 5-7 minutes, until softened.

3 Add the tomatoes and oregano to the pan and then season to taste with salt and pepper. Lower the heat and simmer for 10-12 minutes.

4 Bring a large pan of lightly salted water to the boil. Add the orecchiette and oil and cook for 12 minutes, until just tender, but still firm to the bite. Drain the pasta and transfer to a warm serving dish or bowl. Spoon over the bacon and tomato sauce, toss to coat and serve with the cheese.

VARIATION

You could also use 450 g/1 lb spicy Italian sausages. Squeeze the meat out of the skins and add to the pan in step 2 instead of the bacon.

COOK'S TIP

For an authentic Italian flavour use pancetta, rather than ordinary bacon. This kind of bacon is streaked with fat and adds rich undertones of flavour to many traditional dishes. It is available both smoked and unsmoked and can be bought in a single, large piece or cut into slices. You can buy it in some supermarkets and all Italian delicatessens.

Marinated Aubergine (Eggplant) on a Bed of Linguine

This unusual, fruity marinade makes the aubergine (eggplant) slices simply melt in the mouth.

Serves 4

INGREDIENTS

150 ml/¼ pint/⅝ cup
vegetable stock
150 ml/¼ pint/⅝ cup white
wine vinegar
2 tsp balsamic vinegar
3 tbsp olive oil
fresh oregano sprig

450 g/1 lb aubergine (eggplant),
peeled and thinly sliced
400 g/14 oz dried linguine

MARINADE:
2 tbsp extra virgin oil
2 garlic cloves, crushed

2 tbsp chopped fresh oregano
2 tbsp finely chopped
roasted almonds
2 tbsp diced red (bell) pepper
2 tbsp lime juice
grated rind and juice of 1 orange
salt and pepper

1 Put the vegetable stock, wine vinegar and balsamic vinegar into a saucepan and bring to the boil over a low heat. Add 2 tsp of the olive oil and the sprig of oregano and simmer gently for about 1 minute.

2 Add the aubergine (eggplant) slices to the pan, remove from the heat and set aside for 10 minutes.

3 Meanwhile make the marinade. Combine the oil, garlic, fresh oregano, almonds, (bell) pepper, lime juice, orange rind and juice together in a large bowl and season to taste.

4 Carefully remove the aubergine (eggplant) from the saucepan with a slotted spoon, and drain well. Add the aubergine (eggplant) slices to the marinade,

mixing well, and set aside in the refrigerator for about 12 hours.

5 Bring a large pan of lightly salted water to the boil. Add half the remaining oil and the linguine and cook until just tender. Drain the pasta and toss with the remaining oil while still warm. Arrange the pasta on a serving plate with the aubergine (eggplant) slices and the marinade and serve.

Spinach & Ricotta Shells

*This is a classic combination in which the smooth, creamy
cheese balances the sharper taste of the spinach.*

Serves 4

INGREDIENTS

400 g/14 oz dried lumache
rigate grande
5 tbsp olive oil
60/g 2 oz/1 cup fresh
white breadcrumbs

125 ml/4 fl oz/^{1}/$_2$ cup milk
300 g/10^1/$_2$ oz frozen spinach,
thawed and drained
225 g/8 oz/1 cup ricotta cheese
pinch of freshly grated nutmeg

400 g/14 oz can chopped
tomatoes, drained
1 garlic clove, crushed
salt and pepper

1 Bring a large saucepan of
lightly salted water to the
boil. Add the lumache and 1 tbsp
of the olive oil and cook until just
tender, but still firm to the bite.
Drain the pasta, refresh under
cold water and set aside.

2 Put the breadcrumbs, milk
and 3 tbsp of the remaining
olive oil in a food processor and
work to combine.

3 Add the spinach and ricotta
cheese to the food processor
and work to a smooth mixture.

Transfer to a bowl, stir in the
nutmeg, and season with salt and
pepper to taste.

4 Mix together the tomatoes,
garlic and remaining oil and
spoon the mixture into the base of
an ovenproof dish.

5 Using a teaspoon, fill the
lumache with the spinach and
ricotta mixture and arrange on top
of the tomato mixture in the dish.
Cover and bake in a preheated
oven at 180°C/350°F/Gas 4 for 20
minutes. Serve hot.

COOK'S TIP

*Ricotta is a creamy Italian cheese
traditionally made from ewes' milk
whey. It is soft and white, with a
smooth texture and a slightly sweet
flavour. It should be used within
2–3 days of purchase.*

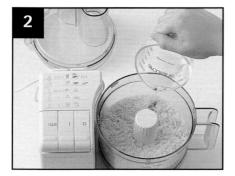

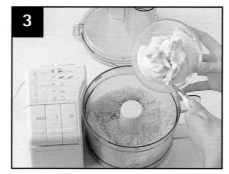

Rotelle with Spicy Italian Sauce

This filling vegetarian dish is perfect for an inexpensive and quick lunch.

Serves 4

INGREDIENTS

5 tbsp olive oil
3 garlic cloves, crushed
2 fresh red chillies, chopped

1 green chilli, chopped
200 ml/7 fl oz/⁷⁄₈ cup Italian Red Wine Sauce (see Cook's Tip)

400 g/14 oz/3¹⁄₂ cups dried rotelle
salt and pepper
warm Italian bread, to serve

1 Make the Italian Red Wine Sauce (see Cook's Tip, right).

2 Heat 4 tbsp of the oil in a saucepan. Add the garlic and chillies and fry for 3 minutes.

3 Stir in the Italian Red Wine Sauce (see Cook's Tip, right), season with salt and pepper to taste, and simmer gently over a low heat for 20 minutes.

4 Bring a large saucepan of lightly salted water to the boil. Add the rotelle and the remaining oil and cook for 8 minutes, until just tender, but still firm to the bite. Drain the pasta.

5 Toss the rotelle in the spicy sauce, transfer to a warm serving dish and serve with warm Italian bread.

COOK'S TIP

Take care when using fresh chillies as they can burn your skin. Handle them as little as possible – wear rubber gloves if necessary. Always wash your hands thoroughly afterwards and don't touch your face or eyes before you have washed your hands. Remove chilli seeds before chopping the chillies, as they are the hottest part, and shouldn't be allowed to slip into the food.

COOK'S TIP

To make Italian Red Wine Sauce, first make a demi-glace sauce by combining 150 ml/¹⁄₄ pint/⁵⁄₈ cup each Brown Stock (see page 28) and Espagnole Sauce (see page 14), cook for 10 minutes and strain. Meanwhile, combine 125 ml/4 fl oz/¹⁄₂ cup red wine, 2 tbsp red wine vinegar, 4 tbsp chopped shallots, 1 bay leaf and 1 thyme sprig in a small saucepan. Bring to the boil and reduce by about three-quarters. Add the demi-glace sauce and simmer for 20 minutes. Season with pepper and strain.

Tricolour Timballini

An unusual way of serving pasta, these cheese moulds
are excellent with a crunchy salad for a light lunch.

Serves 4

INGREDIENTS

15 g/^{1}/$_2$ oz/1 tbsp butter, softened
60 g/2 oz/1 cup dried white
　breadcrumbs
175 g/6 oz dried tricolour spaghetti,
　broken into 5 cm/2 inch lengths
3 tbsp olive oil
300 ml/^{1}/$_2$ pint/1^1/$_4$ cups Béchamel
　Sauce (see page 166)

1 egg yolk
125 g/4 oz/1 cup grated Gruyère
　(Swiss) cheese
1 onion, finely chopped
1 bay leaf
150 ml/^{1}/$_4$ pint/^{5}/$_8$ cup dry
　white wine

150 ml/^{1}/$_4$ pint/^{5}/$_8$ cup passata
　(sieved tomatoes)
1 tbsp tomato purée (paste)
salt and pepper
fresh basil leaves, to garnish

1　Grease four 180 ml/6 fl oz/
　^{3}/$_4$ cup moulds or ramekins
with the butter. Evenly coat the
insides with half the breadcrumbs.

2　Bring a saucepan of lightly
　salted water to the boil. Add
the spaghetti and 1 tbsp of the oil
and cook until just tender. Drain
and transfer to a mixing bowl.

3　Add the egg yolk and cheese
　to the pasta and season. Pour

the Béchamel sauce into the bowl
and mix. Spoon the mixture into
the ramekins and sprinkle over the
remaining breadcrumbs.

4　Stand the ramekins on a
　baking (cookie) sheet and
bake in a preheated oven at 220°C/
425°F/Gas 7 for 20 minutes. Set
aside for 10 minutes.

5　Meanwhile, make the sauce.
　Heat the remaining oil in a

pan and gently fry the onion and
bay leaf for 2-3 minutes.

6　Stir in the wine, passata
　(sieved tomatoes) and tomato
purée (paste) and season. Simmer
for 20 minutes, until thickened.
Remove and discard the bay leaf.

7　Turn the timballini out on to
　individual serving plates,
garnish with the basil leaves and
serve with the tomato sauce.

Tagliarini with Gorgonzola

This simple, creamy pasta sauce is a classic Italian recipe.

Serves 4

INGREDIENTS

25 g/1 oz/2 tbsp butter
225 g/8 oz Gorgonzola cheese,
    roughly crumbled
150 ml/¼ pint/⅝ cup double
    (heavy) cream

30 ml/2 tbsp dry white wine
1 tsp cornflour (cornstarch)
4 fresh sage sprigs, finely chopped
400 g/14 oz dried tagliarini
2 tbsp olive oil

salt and white pepper

1 Melt the butter in a heavy-based saucepan. Stir in 175 g/6 oz of the Gorgonzola cheese and melt, over a low heat, for about 2 minutes.

2 Add the cream, wine and cornflour (cornstarch) and beat with a whisk until fully incorporated.

3 Stir in the sage and season to taste with salt and white pepper. Bring to the boil over a low heat, whisking constantly, until the sauce thickens. Remove from the heat and set aside while you cook the pasta.

4 Bring a large saucepan of lightly salted water to the boil. Add the tagliarini and 1 tbsp of the olive oil. Cook the pasta for 12–14 minutes or until just tender, drain thoroughly and toss in the remaining olive oil. Transfer the pasta to a serving dish and keep warm.

5 Return the saucepan containing the sauce to a low heat to reheat the sauce, whisking constantly. Spoon the Gorgonzola sauce over the tagliarini, generously sprinkle over the remaining cheese and serve immediately.

COOK'S TIP

Gorgonzola is one of the world's oldest veined cheeses and, arguably, its finest. When buying, always check that it is creamy yellow with delicate green veining. Avoid hard or discoloured cheese. It should have a rich, piquant aroma, not a bitter smell. If you find Gorgonzola too strong or rich, you could substitute Danish blue.

Gnocchi Piemontese

*Gnocchi, a speciality from northern Italy, are small
dumplings that are either poached or baked.*

Serves 4

INGREDIENTS

450 g/1 lb warm mashed potato
75 g/2³/₄ oz/⁵/₈ cup self-raising
   (self-rising) flour
1 egg

2 egg yolks
1 tbsp olive oil
150 ml/¹/₄ pint/⁵/₈ cup Espagnole
   Sauce (see page 14)

60 g/2 oz/4 tbsp butter
175 g/6 oz/2 cups freshly grated
   Parmesan cheese
salt and pepper

1 In a large bowl, mix together the mashed potato and flour. Add the egg and egg yolks, season well with salt and pepper and mix together to form a dough.

2 Break off pieces of the dough and roll between the palms of your hands to form small balls the size of a walnut. Flatten the balls with a fork into the shape of small cylinders.

3 Bring a large pan of lightly salted water to the boil. Add the gnocchi and olive oil and poach for 10 minutes.

4 Mix the Espagnole sauce (see page 14) and the butter in a large saucepan over a gentle heat. Gradually blend in the grated Parmesan cheese.

5 Remove the gnocchi from the pan with a slotted spoon. Toss the gnocchi in the sauce, transfer to 4 individual serving plates and serve immediately.

COOK'S TIP

This dish also makes an excellent main meal with a crisp salad.

VARIATION

These gnocchi would also taste delicious with a tomato sauce, in Trentino-style. Mix together 115 g/4 oz/1 cup finely chopped sun-dried tomatoes, 1 finely sliced celery stick (stalk), 1 crushed garlic clove and 6 tbsp red wine in a pan. Cook over a low heat for 15–20 minutes. Stir in 8 skinned, chopped, Italian plum tomatoes, season to taste with salt and pepper and simmer over a low heat for a further 10 minutes.

Pasta Omelette

This is a superb way of using up any leftover pasta,
such as penne, macaroni or conchiglie.

Serves 2

INGREDIENTS

4 tbsp olive oil
1 small onion, chopped
1 fennel bulb, thinly sliced
125 g/4^1/$_2$ oz potato, diced
1 garlic clove, chopped

4 eggs
1 tbsp chopped fresh flat leaf parsley
pinch of chilli powder
100 g/3^1/$_2$ oz cooked short pasta
2 tbsp stuffed green olives, halved

salt and pepper
fresh marjoram sprigs, to garnish
tomato salad, to serve

1 Heat half the oil in a heavy-based frying pan (skillet) over a low heat. Add the onion, fennel and potato and fry, stirring occasionally, for 8-10 minutes, until the potato is just tender.

2 Stir in the garlic and cook for 1 minute. Remove the pan from the heat and transfer the vegetables to a plate and set aside.

3 Beat the eggs until they are frothy. Stir in the parsley and season with salt, pepper and a pinch of chilli powder.

4 Heat 1 tbsp of the remaining oil in a clean frying pan (skillet). Add half of the egg mixture to the pan, then add the cooked vegetables, pasta and half of the olives. Pour in the remaining egg mixture and cook until the sides begin to set.

5 Lift up the edges of the omelette with a palette knife (spatula) to allow the uncooked egg to spread underneath. Cook, shaking the pan occasionally, until the underside is a light golden brown colour.

6 Slide the omelette out of the pan on to a plate. Wipe the pan with kitchen paper (kitchen towels) and heat the remaining oil. Invert the omelette into the pan and cook until the other side is golden brown.

7 Slide the omelette on to a warmed serving dish and garnish with the remaining olives and the marjoram. Serve cut into wedges, with a tomato salad.

Spaghetti with Ricotta Cheese

*This light pasta dish has a delicate flavour
ideally suited to a summer lunch.*

Serves 4

INGREDIENTS

350 g/12 oz dried spaghetti
3 tbsp olive oil
40 g/^{1}/2 oz/3 tbsp butter
2 tbsp chopped fresh flat leaf parsley
125 g/4^1/2 oz/1 cup freshly
  ground almonds

125 g/4^1/2 oz/^{1}/2 cup ricotta cheese
pinch of grated nutmeg
pinch of ground cinnamon
150 ml/^{1}/4 pint/^{5}/8 cup crème fraîche
  (unsweetened yogurt)
125 ml/4 fl oz hot chicken stock

1 tbsp pine nuts (kernels)
salt and pepper
fresh flat leaf parsley sprigs,
  to garnish

1 Bring a large pan of lightly salted water to the boil. Add the spaghetti and 1 tbsp of the oil and cook until tender, but still firm to the bite.

2 Drain the pasta, return to the pan and toss with the butter and chopped parsley. Set aside and keep warm.

3 To make the sauce, mix together the ground almonds, ricotta cheese, nutmeg, cinnamon and crème fraîche (unsweetened yogurt) over a low heat to form a thick paste. Gradually stir in the remaining oil. When the oil has been fully incorporated, gradually stir in the hot chicken stock, until smooth. Season to taste with black pepper.

4 Transfer the spaghetti to a warm serving dish, pour over the sauce and toss together well (see Cook's Tip, right). Sprinkle over the pine nuts (kernels), garnish with the flat leaf parsley and serve warm.

COOK'S TIP

*Use two large forks to toss spaghetti
or other long pasta, so that it is
thoroughly coated with the sauce.
Special spaghetti forks are available
from some cookware departments
and kitchen shops. Holding one
fork in each hand, gently ease the
prongs under the pasta on each side
and lift them towards the centre.
Continue this evenly and
rhythmically until the pasta is
completely coated.*

Gnocchi Romana

This is a traditional recipe but, for a less rich version, omit the eggs.

Serves 4

INGREDIENTS

700 ml/1¼ pints/3⅛ cups milk
pinch of freshly grated nutmeg
90 g/3 oz/6 tbsp butter, plus extra
   for greasing

250 g/8 oz/1¼ cups semolina
125 g/4½ oz/1½ cups grated
   Parmesan cheese
2 eggs, beaten

60 g/2 oz/½ cup grated Gruyère
   (Swiss) cheese
salt and pepper
fresh basil sprigs, to garnish

1 Pour the milk into a saucepan and bring to the boil. Remove the pan from the heat and stir in the nutmeg, 25 g/1 oz/2 tbsp of the butter and salt and pepper to taste.

2 Gradually stir the semolina into the milk, whisking to prevent lumps forming, and return the pan to a low heat. Simmer, stirring constantly, for about 10 minutes, until very thick.

3 Beat 60 g/2 oz/⅔ cup of Parmesan cheese into the semolina mixture, then beat in the eggs. Continue beating the mixture until smooth. Set the mixture aside for a few minutes to cool slightly.

4 Spread out the semolina mixture in an even layer on a sheet of baking parchment or in a large, oiled baking tin (pan), smoothing the surface with a damp spatula – it should be about 1 cm/½ inch thick. Set aside to cool completely, then leave to chill in the refrigerator for 1 hour.

5 Once chilled, cut out rounds of gnocchi, measuring about 4 cm/1½ inches in diameter, using a plain, greased pastry cutter.

6 Grease a shallow ovenproof dish or 4 individual dishes. Lay the gnocchi trimmings in the base of the dish or dishes and cover with overlapping rounds of gnocchi.

7 Melt the remaining butter and drizzle over the gnocchi. Sprinkle over the remaining Parmesan cheese, then sprinkle over the Gruyère (Swiss) cheese.

8 Bake in a preheated oven at 200°C/400°F/Gas 6 for 25-30 minutes, until the top is crisp and golden brown. Serve hot, garnished with the basil.

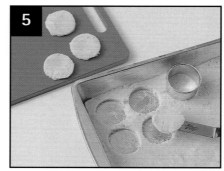

Three Cheese Bake

Serve this dish while the cheese is still hot and melted, as cooked cheese turns very rubbery if it is allowed to cool down.

Serves 4

INGREDIENTS

butter, for greasing
400 g/14 oz dried penne
1 tbsp olive oil
2 eggs, beaten

350 g/12 oz/1$^{1}/_{2}$ cups ricotta cheese
4 fresh basil sprigs
100 g/3$^{1}/_{2}$ oz/1 cup grated
  mozzarella or halloumi cheese

4 tbsp freshly grated
  Parmesan cheese
salt and black pepper
fresh basil leaves (optional), to garnish

1 Lightly grease an ovenproof dish with butter.

2 Bring a large pan of lightly salted water to the boil. Add the penne and olive oil and cook until just tender, but still firm to the bite. Drain the pasta, set aside and keep warm.

3 Beat the eggs into the ricotta cheese and season to taste with salt and pepper.

4 Spoon half of the penne into the base of the dish and cover with half of the basil leaves.

5 Spoon over half of the ricotta cheese mixture. Sprinkle over the mozzarella or halloumi cheese and top with the remaining basil leaves. Cover with the remaining penne and then spoon over the remaining ricotta cheese mixture. Lightly sprinkle over the grated Parmesan cheese.

6 Bake in a preheated oven at 190°C/375°F/Gas 5 for 30–40 minutes, until golden brown and the cheese topping is hot and bubbling. Garnish with fresh basil leaves, if liked, and serve hot.

VARIATION

Try substituting smoked Bavarian cheese for the mozzarella or halloumi and grated Cheddar cheese for the Parmesan, for a slightly different but just as delicious flavour.

Baked Rigatoni Filled with Tuna & Ricotta Cheese

Ribbed tubes of pasta are filled with fish and cheese and then baked in a creamy sauce.

Serves 4

INGREDIENTS

butter, for greasing
450 g/1 lb dried rigatoni
1 tbsp olive oil
200 g /7 oz can flaked tuna, drained

225 g/ 8 oz ricotta cheese
125 ml/4 fl oz/$^{1}/_{2}$ cup double (heavy) cream
225 g/8 oz/2$^{2}/_{3}$ cups grated Parmesan cheese

125 g/4 oz sun-dried tomatoes, drained and sliced
salt and pepper

1 Lightly grease an ovenproof dish with butter.

2 Bring a large saucepan of lightly salted water to the boil. Add the rigatoni and olive oil and cook until just tender, but still firm to the bite. Drain the pasta and set aside until cool enough to handle.

3 In a bowl, mix together the tuna and ricotta cheese to form a soft paste. Spoon the mixture into a piping bag and use to fill the rigatoni. Arrange the filled pasta tubes side by side in the prepared ovenproof dish.

4 To make the sauce, mix the cream and Parmesan cheese and season. Spoon the sauce over the rigatoni and top with the sun-dried tomatoes arranged in a criss-cross pattern. Bake in a preheated oven at 200°C/400°F/Gas 6 for 20 minutes. Serve hot straight from the dish.

VARIATION

For a vegetarian alternative of this recipe, simply substitute a mixture of stoned (pitted) and chopped black olives and chopped walnuts for the tuna. Follow exactly the same cooking method.

Spaghetti with Anchovy & Pesto Sauce

This is an ideal dish for cooks in a hurry and for those who do not have much time for shopping, as it is prepared in minutes from store-cupboard ingredients.

Serves 4

INGREDIENTS

90 ml/3 fl oz olive oil
2 garlic cloves, crushed
60 g/2 oz can anchovy fillets, drained
450 g/1 lb dried spaghetti
60 g/2 oz Pesto Sauce (see page 12)

2 tbsp finely chopped fresh oregano
90 g/3 oz/1 cup grated Parmesan
cheese, plus extra for
serving (optional)

salt and pepper
2 fresh oregano sprigs, to garnish

1 Reserve 1 tbsp of the oil and heat the remainder in a small saucepan. Add the garlic and fry for 3 minutes.

2 Lower the heat, stir in the anchovies and cook, stirring occasionally, until the anchovies have disintegrated.

3 Bring a large saucepan of lightly salted water to the boil. Add the spaghetti and the remaining olive oil and cook until just tender, but still firm to the bite.

4 Add the Pesto Sauce (see page 12) and chopped fresh oregano to the anchovy mixture and then season with black pepper to taste.

5 Drain the spaghetti, using a slotted spoon, and transfer to a warm serving dish. Pour the Pesto Sauce over the spaghetti and then sprinkle over the grated Parmesan cheese.

6 Garnish with oregano sprigs and serve with extra cheese, if using.

VARIATION

For a vegetarian alternative of this recipe, simply substitute drained sun-dried tomatoes for the anchovy fillets.

COOK'S TIP

If you find canned anchovies much too salty, soak them in a saucer of cold milk for 5 minutes, drain and pat dry with kitchen paper (kitchen towels) before using.

Fettuccine with Anchovy & Spinach Sauce

This colourful starter can be made with a variety of different pasta, including spaghetti and linguine.

Serves 4

INGREDIENTS

900 g/2 lb fresh, young
   spinach leaves
400 g/14 oz dried fettuccine

6 tbsp olive oil
3 tbsp pine nuts (kernels)
3 garlic cloves, crushed

8 canned anchovy fillets, drained
   and chopped
salt

1 Trim off any tough spinach stalks. Rinse the spinach leaves and place them in a large saucepan with only the water that is clinging to them after washing. Cover and cook over a high heat, shaking the pan from time, until the spinach has wilted, but retains its colour. Drain well, set aside and keep warm.

2 Bring a large saucepan of lightly salted water to the boil. Add the fettuccine and 1 tbsp of the oil and cook until it is just tender, but still firm to the bite.

3 Heat 4 tbsp of the remaining oil in a saucepan. Add the pine nuts (kernels) and fry until golden. Remove from the pan and set aside.

4 Add the garlic to the pan and fry until golden. Add the anchovies and stir in the spinach. Cook, stirring, for 2-3 minutes, until heated through. Return the pine nuts (kernels) to the pan.

5 Drain the fettuccine, toss in the remaining olive oil and transfer to a warm serving dish.

Spoon the anchovy and spinach sauce over the fettucine, toss lightly and serve immediately.

COOK'S TIP

If you are in a hurry, you can use frozen spinach. Thaw and drain it thoroughly, pressing out as much moisture as possible. Cut the leaves into strips and add to the dish with the anchovies in step 4.

Penne with Muscoli Fritti nell' Olio

*This is quick and simple, but one of the nicest
of Italian fried fish dishes, served with penne.*

Serves 4–6

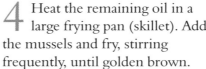

INGREDIENTS

400/14 oz 3^1/$_2$ cups dried penne
125 ml/4 fl oz/^{1}/$_2$ cup olive oil
450 g/1 lb mussels, cooked
 and shelled

1 tsp sea salt
90 g/3 oz/^{2}/$_3$ cup flour
100 g/3^1/$_2$ oz sun-dried
 tomatoes, sliced

2 tbsp chopped fresh basil leaves
salt and pepper
1 lemon, thinly sliced, to garnish

1 Bring a large saucepan of lightly salted water to the boil. Add the penne and 1 tbsp of the olive oil and cook until the pasta is just tender, but still firm to the bite.

2 Drain the pasta well and place in a large, warm serving dish. Set aside and keep warm while you cook the mussels.

3 Lightly sprinkle the mussels with the sea salt. Season the flour with salt and pepper to taste, sprinkle into a bowl and toss the mussels in the flour until coated.

4 Heat the remaining oil in a large frying pan (skillet). Add the mussels and fry, stirring frequently, until golden brown.

5 Toss the mussels with the penne and sprinkle with the sun-dried tomatoes and basil leaves. Garnish with slices of lemon and serve immediately.

VARIATION

You could substitute clams for the mussels. If using fresh clams, try smaller varieties, such as Venus.

COOK'S TIP

Sun-dried tomatoes have been used in Mediterranean countries for a long time, but have become popular elsewhere only quite recently. They are dried and then preserved in oil. They have a concentrated, almost roasted flavour and a dense texture. They should be drained and chopped or sliced before using.

Meat & Poultry

Pasta and meat or poultry is a classic combination. Dishes range from easy, economic mid-week suppers to sophisticated and elegant meals for special occasions. The recipes in this chapter include many family favourites, such as Spaghetti Bolognese, Fresh Spaghetti with Italian Meatballs in Tomato Sauce, Lasagne Verde and Stuffed Cannelloni. There are also some exciting variations on traditional themes, such as Sicilian Spaghetti, Beef & Pasta Bake and Stir-fried Pork with Pasta & Vegetables. Finally, there is a superb collection of mouth-watering original recipes. Why not try Fettuccine with Fillet of Veal & Pink Grapefruit in a Rose Petal Butter Sauce, Orecchioni with Pork in Cream Sauce, garnished with Quail Eggs, Chicken & Lobster on a Bed of Penne, or Rigatoni & Pesto Baked Partridge? You will be astonished at how quickly and easily you can prepare these gourmet dishes.

Spaghetti Bolognese

*You can use this classic meat sauce for lasagne, cannelloni
or any other baked pasta dishes.*

Serves 4

INGREDIENTS

3 tbsp olive oil
2 garlic cloves, crushed
1 large onion, finely chopped
1 carrot, diced
225 g/8 oz/2 cups lean minced
  (ground) beef, veal or chicken

85 g/3 oz chicken livers,
  finely chopped
100 g/3^1/$_2$ oz lean, Parma ham
  (prosciutto), diced
150 ml/^{1}/$_4$ pint/^{5}/$_8$ cup Marsala

285 g/10 oz can chopped
  plum tomatoes
1 tbsp chopped fresh basil leaves
2 tbsp tomato purée (paste)
salt and pepper
450 g/1 lb dried spaghetti

1 Heat 2 tbsp of the olive oil in a large saucepan. Add the garlic, onion and carrot and fry for 6 minutes.

2 Add the minced (ground) beef, veal or chicken, chicken livers and Parma ham (prosciutto) to the pan and cook over a medium heat for 12 minutes, until well browned.

3 Stir in the Marsala, tomatoes, basil and tomato purée (paste) and cook for 4 minutes. Season to taste with salt and pepper. Cover and simmer for about 30 minutes.

4 Remove the lid from the pan, stir and simmer for a further 15 minutes.

5 Meanwhile, bring a large pan of lightly salted water to the boil. Add the spaghetti and the remaining oil and cook for about 12 minutes, until tender, but still firm to the bite. Drain and transfer to a serving dish. Pour the sauce over the pasta, toss and serve hot.

VARIATION

Chicken livers are an essential ingredient in a classic Bolognese sauce to which they add richness. However, if you prefer not to use them, you can substitute the same quantity of minced (ground) beef.

Creamed Strips of Sirloin with Rigatoni

*This quick and easy dish tastes superb and would
make a delicious treat for a special occasion.*

Serves 4

INGREDIENTS

75 g/3 oz/6 tbsp butter
450 g/1 lb sirloin steak, trimmed and
   cut into thin strips
175 g/6 oz button mushrooms, sliced
1 tsp mustard
pinch of freshly grated root ginger

2 tbsp dry sherry
150 ml/$^1/_4$ pint/$^5/_8$ cup double
   (heavy) cream
salt and pepper
4 slices hot toast, cut into triangles,
   to serve

PASTA:
450 g/1 lb dried rigatoni
2 tbsp olive oil
2 fresh basil sprigs
115 g/4 oz/8 tbsp butter

1 Preheat the oven to
90°C/375°F/Gas 5. Melt the
butter in a large frying pan
(skillet) and gently fry the steak
over a low heat, stirring
frequently, for 6 minutes. Using a
slotted spoon, transfer the steak to
an ovenproof dish and keep warm.

2 Add the sliced mushrooms to
the frying pan (skillet) and
cook for 2–3 minutes in the juices
remaining in the pan. Add the
mustard, ginger, salt and pepper.
Cook for 2 minutes, then add the

sherry and cream. Cook for a
further 3 minutes, then pour the
cream sauce over the steak.

3 Bake the steak and cream
mixture in the preheated oven
for 10 minutes.

4 Meanwhile, cook the pasta.
Bring a large saucepan of
lightly salted water to the boil. Add
the rigatoni, olive oil and 1 of the
basil sprigs and boil rapidly for
10 minutes, until tender but still
firm to the bite. Drain the pasta

and transfer to a warm serving
plate. Toss the pasta with the
butter and garnish with a sprig
of basil.

5 Serve the steak with the pasta
and triangles of warm toast.

COOK'S TIP

*Dried pasta will keep for up to 6
months. Keep it in the packet and
reseal it once you have opened it, or
transfer the pasta to an airtight jar.*

Fresh Spaghetti with Italian Meatballs in Tomato Sauce

This well-loved Italian dish is famous across the world. Make the most of it by using high-quality steak for the meatballs.

Serves 4

INGREDIENTS

150 g/5¹/2 oz/2¹/2 cups brown breadcrumbs
150 ml/¹/4 pint/⁵/8 cup milk
25 g/1 oz/2 tbsp butter
25 g/1 oz/¹/4 cup wholemeal (whole-wheat) flour

200 ml/7 fl oz/⁷/8 cup beef stock
400 g/14 oz can chopped tomatoes
2 tbsp tomato purée (paste)
1 tsp sugar
1 tbsp finely chopped fresh tarragon
1 large onion, chopped

450 g/1 lb/4 cups minced steak
1 tsp paprika
4 tbsp olive oil
450 g/1 lb fresh spaghetti
salt and pepper
fresh tarragon sprigs, to garnish

1 Place the breadcrumbs in a bowl, add the milk and set aside to soak for 30 minutes.

2 Melt half the butter in a pan. Add the flour and cook, stirring constantly, for 2 minutes. Gradually stir in the beef stock and cook, stirring constantly, for a further 5 minutes. Add the tomatoes, tomato purée (paste), sugar and tarragon. Season well and simmer for 25 minutes.

3 Mix the onion, steak and paprika into the breadcrumbs and season to taste. Shape the mixture into 14 meatballs.

4 Heat the oil and remaining butter in a frying pan (skillet) and fry the meatballs, turning frequently, until brown all over. Place them in a deep casserole, pour over the tomato sauce, cover and bake in a preheated oven at 180°C/350°F/Gas 4 for 25 minutes.

5 Bring a large saucepan of lightly salted water to the boil. Add the fresh spaghetti, bring back to the boil and cook for about 2–3 minutes, until tender, but still firm to the bite.

6 Meanwhile, remove the meatballs from the oven and allow them to cool for 3 minutes. Serve the meatballs and their sauce with the spaghetti, garnished with tarragon sprigs.

Egg Noodles with Beef

*Quick and easy, this mouth-watering Chinese-style
noodle dish can be cooked in minutes.*

Serves 4

INGREDIENTS

285 g/10 oz egg noodles
3 tbsp walnut oil
2.5 cm/1 inch piece fresh root ginger,
   cut into thin strips
5 spring onions (scallions),
   finely shredded
2 garlic cloves, finely chopped

1 red (bell) pepper, cored, seeded and
   thinly sliced
100 g/3^1/$_2$ oz button mushrooms,
   thinly sliced
340 g/12 oz fillet steak, cut into
   thin strips
1 tbsp cornflour (cornstarch)

5 tbsp dry sherry
3 tbsp soy sauce
1 tsp soft brown sugar
225 g/8 oz/1 cup beansprouts
1 tbsp sesame oil
salt and pepper
spring onion (scallion) strips, to garnish

1 Bring a large saucepan of water to the boil. Add the noodles and cook according to the instructions on the packet. Drain the noodles and set aside.

2 Heat the walnut oil in a preheated wok. Add the ginger, spring onions (scallions) and garlic and stir-fry for 45 seconds. Add the (bell) pepper, mushrooms and steak and stir-fry for 4 minutes. Season to taste with salt and pepper.

3 Mix together the cornflour (cornstarch), sherry and soy sauce in a small jug to form a paste, and pour into the wok. Sprinkle over the brown sugar and stir-fry all of the ingredients for a further 2 minutes.

4 Add the beansprouts, drained noodles and sesame oil to the wok, stir and toss together for 1 minute. Garnish with strips of spring onion (scallion) and serve immediately.

COOK'S TIP

If you do not have a wok, you could prepare this dish in a frying pan (skillet). However, a wok is preferable, as the round base ensures an even distribution of heat and it is easier to keep stirring and tossing the contents when stir-frying.

Tagliarini with Meatballs in Red Wine & Oyster Mushroom Sauce

A different twist is given to this traditional pasta dish with a rich, but subtle, sauce.

Serves 4

INGREDIENTS

150 g/5 oz/2 cups white breadcrumbs
150 ml/^{1}/$_4$ pint/^{5}/$_8$ cup milk
25 g/1 oz/2 tbsp butter
9 tbsp olive oil
225 g/8 oz/3 cups sliced
  oyster mushrooms
25 g/1 oz/^{1}/$_4$ cup wholemeal
  (whole-wheat) flour

200 ml/7 fl oz/^{7}/$_8$ cup beef stock
150 ml/^{1}/$_4$ pint/^{5}/$_8$ cup red wine
4 tomatoes, skinned and chopped
1 tbsp tomato purée (paste)
1 tsp brown sugar
1 tbsp finely chopped fresh basil
12 shallots, chopped

450 g/1 lb/4 cups minced
  (ground) steak
1 tsp paprika
450 g/1 lb dried egg tagliarini
salt and pepper
fresh basil sprigs, to garnish

1 Soak the breadcrumbs in the milk for 30 minutes.

2 Heat half the butter and 4 tbsp of the oil in a pan. Fry the mushrooms for 4 minutes, then stir in the flour and cook for 2 minutes. Add the stock and wine and simmer for 15 minutes. Add the tomatoes, tomato purée (paste), sugar and basil. Season well and simmer for 30 minutes.

3 Mix the shallots, steak and paprika with the breadcrumbs and season. Shape the mixture into 14 meatballs.

4 Heat 4 tbsp of the remaining oil and the remaining butter in a large frying pan (skillet). Fry the meatballs, turning frequently, until brown all over. Transfer to a deep casserole, pour over the red wine and the mushroom sauce, cover

and bake in a preheated oven at 180°C/350°F/Gas 4 for 30 minutes.

5 Bring a pan of salted water to the boil. Add the pasta and the remaining oil and cook until tender. Drain and transfer to a serving dish. Remove the casserole from the oven and cool for 3 minutes. Pour the meatballs and sauce on to the pasta, garnish with the basil sprigs and serve.

Sicilian Spaghetti

This delicious Sicilian dish originated as a handy way of using up leftover cooked pasta.

Serves 4

INGREDIENTS

150 ml/^{1}/4 pint/^{5}/8 cup olive oil, plus
   extra for brushing
2 aubergines (eggplant)
350 g/12 oz/3 cups minced
   (ground) beef
1 onion, chopped
2 garlic cloves, crushed
2 tbsp tomato purée (paste)
400 g/14 oz can chopped tomatoes

1 tsp Worcestershire sauce
1 tsp chopped fresh marjoram or
   oregano or ^{1}/2 tsp dried marjoram
   or oregano
60 g/2 oz/^{1}/2 cup stoned (pitted)
   black olives, sliced
1 green, red or yellow (bell) pepper,
   cored, seeded and chopped
175 g/6 oz dried spaghetti

115 g/4 oz/1 cup freshly grated
   Parmesan cheese
salt and pepper
fresh oregano or parsley sprigs,
   to garnish

1 Brush a 20 cm/8 inch loose-based round cake tin (pan) with oil, line the base with baking parchment and brush with oil.

2 Slice the aubergines (eggplant). Heat a little oil in a pan and fry the aubergines (eggplant) in batches until browned on both sides. Add more oil, as necessary. Drain on kitchen paper (kitchen towels).

3 Put the beef, onion and garlic in a saucepan and cook over a medium heat, stirring, until browned. Add the tomato purée (paste), tomatoes, Worcestershire sauce, marjoram or oregano and salt and pepper. Simmer, stirring occasionally, for 10 minutes. Add the olives and (bell) pepper and cook for a further 10 minutes.

4 Bring a pan of salted water to the boil. Add the spaghetti and 1 tbsp olive oil and cook until tender, but still firm to the bite. Drain and turn the spaghetti into a bowl. Add the meat mixture and cheese and toss with 2 forks.

5 Arrange aubergine (eggplant) slices over the base and up the sides of the tin (pan). Add the spaghetti and then cover with the rest of the aubergine (eggplant) slices. Bake in a preheated oven at 200°C/400°F/ Gas 6 for 40 minutes. Leave to stand for 5 minutes, then invert on to a serving dish. Discard the baking parchment. Garnish with the fresh herbs and serve.

Beef & Pasta Bake

The combination of macaroni and beef korma gives this a really authentic flavour.

Serves 4

INGREDIENTS

900g/2 lb steak, cut into cubes
about 150 ml/¹/₄ pint/⁵/₈ cup
   beef stock
450g/1 lb dried macaroni
300 ml/¹/₂ pint/1¹/₄ cups double
   (heavy) cream
¹/₂ tsp garam masala
salt
fresh coriander, to garnish

naan bread, to serve

KORMA PASTE:
60 g/2 oz/¹/₂ cup blanched almonds
6 garlic cloves
2.5 cm/1 inch piece fresh root ginger,
   coarsely chopped
6 tbsp beef stock
1 tsp ground cardamom

4 cloves, crushed
1 tsp cinnamon
2 large onions, chopped
1 tsp coriander seeds
2 tsp ground cumin seeds
pinch of cayenne pepper
6 tbsp of sunflower oil

1 To make the korma paste, grind the almonds finely using a pestle and mortar. Put the ground almonds and the rest of the korma paste ingredients into a food processor or blender and process to make a very smooth paste.

2 Put the steak in a shallow dish and spoon over the korma paste, turning to coat the steak well. Leave in the refrigerator to marinate for 6 hours.

3 Transfer the steak to a large saucepan, and simmer over a low heat, adding a little beef stock if required, for 35 minutes.

4 Meanwhile, bring a large saucepan of lightly salted water to the boil. Add the macaroni and cook for 10 minutes, until tender, but still firm to the bite. Drain the pasta thoroughly and transfer to a deep casserole. Add the steak, double (heavy) cream and garam masala.

5 Bake in a preheated oven at 200°C/400°F/Gas 6 for 30 minutes. Remove the casserole from the oven and allow to stand for about 10 minutes. Garnish the bake with fresh coriander and serve with naan bread.

VARIATION

You could also make this dish using diced chicken and chicken stock, instead of steak and beef stock.

Lasagne Verde

Today you can buy pre-cooked lasagne sheets from most supermarkets; otherwise prepare the lasagne sheets according to the instructions on the packet.

Serves 4–6

INGREDIENTS

butter, for greasing
14 sheets pre-cooked lasagne
850 ml/1^1/$_2$ pints/3^3/$_4$ cups Béchamel Sauce (see page 166)
75 g/3 oz/^{3}/$_4$ cup grated mozzarella cheese
fresh basil (optional), to garnish

MEAT SAUCE:
25 ml/1 fl oz/^{1}/$_8$ cup olive oil
450 g/1 lb/4 cups minced (ground) beef
1 large onion, chopped
1 celery stick (stalk), diced
4 cloves garlic, crushed
25g/1 oz/^{1}/$_4$ cup plain (all purpose) flour

300 ml/^{1}/$_2$ pint/1^1/$_4$ cups beef stock
150 ml/^{1}/$_4$ pint/^{5}/$_8$ cup red wine
1 tbsp chopped fresh parsley
1 tsp chopped fresh marjoram
1 tsp chopped fresh basil
2 tbsp tomato purée (paste)
salt and pepper

1 To make the meat sauce, heat the olive oil in a large frying pan (skillet). Add the minced (ground) beef and fry, stirring frequently, until browned all over. Add the onion, celery and garlic and cook for 3 minutes.

2 Sprinkle over the flour and cook, stirring constantly, for 1 minute. Gradually stir in the stock and red wine, season well with salt and pepper and add the parsley, marjoram and basil. Bring to the boil, lower the heat and simmer for 35 minutes. Add the tomato purée (paste) and simmer for a further 10 minutes.

3 Lightly grease an ovenproof dish with butter. Arrange sheets of lasagne over the base of the dish, spoon over a layer of meat sauce, then Béchamel Sauce.

Place another layer of lasagne on top and repeat the process twice, finishing with a layer of Béchamel Sauce. Sprinkle over the grated mozzarella cheese.

4 Bake the lasagne in a preheated oven at 190°C/375°F/Gas 5 for 35 minutes, until the top is golden brown and bubbling. Garnish with fresh basil, if liked, and serve immediately.

Pasticcio

A recipe with both Italian and Greek origins, this dish
may be served hot or cold, cut into thick satisfying squares.

Serves 6

INGREDIENTS

250 g/8 oz/2 cups dried fusilli
1 tbsp olive oil, plus extra
  for brushing
4 tbsp double (heavy) cream
salt
fresh rosemary sprigs, to garnish
mixed salad, to serve

SAUCE:
2 tbsp olive oil
1 onion, thinly sliced

1 red (bell) pepper, cored, seeded
  and chopped
2 garlic cloves, chopped
600 g/1 lb 5 oz/5^1/4 cups minced
  (ground) beef
400 g/14 oz can chopped tomatoes
125 ml/4 fl oz/^{1}/2 cup dry white wine
2 tbsp chopped fresh parsley
60 g/2 oz can anchovies, drained and
  chopped
salt and pepper

TOPPING:
300 ml/^{1}/2 pint/1^1/4 cups natural
  yogurt
3 eggs
pinch of freshly grated nutmeg
40 g/1^1/2 oz/^{1}/2 cup freshly grated
  Parmesan cheese

---

1 To make the sauce, heat the oil in a frying pan (skillet) and fry the onion and red (bell) pepper for 3 minutes. Add the garlic and cook for 1 minute. Add the beef and cook until browned.

2 Add the tomatoes and wine to the pan and bring to the boil. Lower the heat and simmer for 20 minutes, until thickened.

Stir in the parsley and anchovies and season to taste.

3 Bring a pan of salted water to the boil. Add the pasta and oil and cook for 10 minutes, until almost tender. Drain and transfer to a bowl. Stir in the cream.

4 For the topping, beat the yogurt, eggs and nutmeg.

5 Brush an ovenproof dish with oil. Spoon in half the pasta and cover with half the meat sauce. Repeat, then spread over the topping and sprinkle with cheese.

6 Bake in a preheated oven at 190°C/375°F/Gas 5 for 25 minutes until golden. Garnish with rosemary and serve with a mixed salad.

Fettuccine with Fillet of Veal & Pink Grapefruit in a Rose Petal Butter Sauce

This truly spectacular dish is equally delicious whether you use veal or pork fillet.
Make sure the roses are free of blemishes and pesticides.

Serves 4

INGREDIENTS

450 g/1 lb dried fettuccine
7 tbsp olive oil
1 tsp chopped fresh oregano
1 tsp chopped fresh marjoram
170 g/6 oz/^{3}/4 cup butter
450 g/1 lb veal fillet, thinly sliced

150 ml/^{1}/4 pint/^{5}/8 cup rose petal
  vinegar (see Cook's Tip, below)
150 ml/^{1}/4 pint/^{5}/8 cup fish stock
50 ml/2 fl oz/^{1}/4 cup grapefruit juice
50 ml/2 fl oz/^{1}/4 cup double
  (heavy) cream
salt

TO GARNISH:
12 pink grapefruit segments
12 pink peppercorns
rose petals
fresh herb leaves

1 Bring a pan of lightly salted water to the boil. Add the fettuccine and 1 tbsp of the oil and cook for 12 minutes, until tender, but still firm to the bite. Drain and transfer to a warm serving dish, sprinkle over 2 tbsp of the olive oil, the oregano and marjoram.

2 Heat 50 g/2 oz/4 tbsp of the butter with the remaining oil in a large frying pan (skillet). Add the veal and cook over a low heat for 6 minutes. Remove from the pan and place on top of the pasta.

3 Add the vinegar and fish stock to the pan and bring to the boil. Boil vigorously until reduced by two thirds. Add the grapefruit juice and cream and simmer over a low heat for 4 minutes. Dice the remaining butter and add to the pan, one piece at a time, whisking constantly until it has been completely incorporated.

4 Pour the sauce around the veal, garnish with grapefruit segments, pink peppercorns, the rose petals (washed) and your favourite herb leaves.

COOK'S TIP

To make rose petal vinegar, infuse the petals of 8 pesticide-free roses in 150 ml/^{1}/4 pint/^{5}/8 cup white wine vinegar for 48 hours.

Neapolitan Veal Cutlets with Mascarpone Cheese & Marille

The delicious combination of apple, onion and mushroom perfectly complements the delicate flavour of veal.

Serves 4

INGREDIENTS

200 g/7 oz/⁷/₈ cup butter
4 x 250 g/9 oz veal cutlets, trimmed
1 large onion, sliced
2 apples, peeled, cored and sliced
175 g/ 6 oz button mushrooms
1 tbsp chopped fresh tarragon

8 black peppercorns
1 tbsp sesame seeds
400 g/14 oz dried marille
100 ml/3¹/₂ fl oz/scant ¹/₂ cup extra
   virgin olive oil

175 g/6 oz/³/₄ cup mascarpone
   cheese, broken into small pieces
salt and pepper
2 large beef tomatoes, cut in half
leaves of 1 fresh basil sprig
fresh basil leaves, to garnish

1 Melt 60 g/2 oz/4 tbsp of the butter in a frying pan (skillet). Fry the veal over a low heat for 5 minutes on each side. Transfer to a dish and keep warm.

2 Fry the onion and apples in the pan until lightly browned. Transfer to a dish, place the veal on top and keep warm.

3 Melt the remaining butter in the frying pan (skillet).

Gently fry the mushrooms, tarragon and peppercorns over a low heat for 3 minutes. Sprinkle over the sesame seeds.

4 Bring a pan of salted water to the boil. Add the pasta and 1 tbsp of the oil. Cook until tender, but still firm to the bite. Drain and transfer to a serving plate.

5 Top the pasta with the mascarpone cheese and

sprinkle over the remaining olive oil. Place the onions, apples and veal cutlets on top of the pasta. Spoon the mushrooms, peppercorns and pan juices on to the cutlets, place the tomatoes and basil leaves around the edge and place in a preheated oven at 150°C/ 300°F/Gas 2 for 5 minutes.

6 Season to taste with salt and pepper, garnish with fresh basil leaves and serve immediately.

Stir-fried Pork with Pasta & Vegetables

This delicious dish, with its hint of Thai cuisine,
will certainly get the taste buds tingling.

Serves 4

INGREDIENTS

3 tbsp sesame oil
350 g/12 oz pork fillet (tenderloin),
   cut into thin strips
450 g/1 lb dried taglioni
1 tbsp olive oil
8 shallots, sliced
2 garlic cloves, finely chopped

2.5 cm/1 inch piece fresh root
   ginger, grated
1 fresh green chilli, finely chopped
1 red (bell) pepper, cored, seeded
   and thinly sliced
1 green (bell) pepper, cored, seeded
   and thinly sliced

3 courgettes (zucchini), thinly sliced
2 tbsp ground almonds
1 tsp ground cinnamon
1 tbsp oyster sauce
60 g/2 oz creamed coconut (see
   Cook's Tip, below), grated
salt and pepper

1 Heat the sesame oil in a preheated wok. Season the pork with salt and black pepper, add to the wok and stir-fry for 5 minutes.

2 Meanwhile, bring a large saucepan of lightly salted water to the boil. Add the taglioni and olive oil and cook for about 12 minutes, until just tender, but still firm to the bite. Set the pasta aside and keep warm until required.

3 Add the shallots, garlic, ginger and chilli to the wok and stir-fry for 2 minutes. Add the (bell) peppers and courgettes (zucchini) and stir-fry for 1 minute.

4 Finally, add the ground almonds, cinnamon, oyster sauce and creamed coconut to the wok and stir-fry for 1 minute.

5 Drain the taglioni and transfer to a serving dish. Top with the stir-fry and serve immediately.

COOK'S TIP

Creamed coconut is available from Chinese and Asian food stores and some large supermarkets. It is sold in the form of compressed blocks and adds a concentrated coconut flavour to the dish.

Orecchioni with Pork in Cream Sauce, garnished with Quail Eggs

This unusual and attractive dish is surprisingly quick and easy to make.

Serves 4

INGREDIENTS

450 g/1 lb pork fillet (tenderloin), thinly sliced
4 tbsp olive oil
225 g/8 oz button mushrooms, sliced

200 ml/7 fl oz/^{7}/$_8$ cup Italian Red Wine Sauce (see page 52)
1 tbsp lemon juice
pinch of saffron

350 g/12 oz/3 cups dried orecchioni
4 tbsp double (heavy) cream
12 quail eggs (see Cook's Tip, below)
salt

1 Pound the slices of pork between 2 sheets of clear film (plastic wrap) until they are wafer thin, then cut into strips.

2 Heat the olive oil in a large frying pan (skillet), add the pork and stir-fry for 5 minutes. Add the mushrooms to the pan and stir-fry for a further 2 minutes.

3 Pour over the Italian Red Wine Sauce, lower the heat and simmer gently for 20 minutes.

4 Meanwhile, bring a large saucepan of lightly salted water to the boil. Add the lemon juice, saffron and orecchioni and cook for 12 minutes, until tender but still firm to the bite. Drain the pasta and keep warm.

5 Stir the cream into the pan with the pork and heat gently for a few minutes.

6 Boil the quail eggs for 3 minutes, cool them in cold water and remove the shells.

7 Transfer the pasta to a large, warm serving plate, top with the pork and the sauce and garnish with the eggs. Serve immediately.

COOK'S TIP

In this recipe, the quail eggs are soft-boiled (soft-cooked). As they are extremely difficult to shell when warm, it is important that they are thoroughly cooled first. Otherwise, they will break up unattractively.

Tagliatelle with Pumpkin

This unusual dish comes from the Emilia Romagna region.
Why not serve it with Lambrusco, the local wine?

Serves 4

INGREDIENTS

500 g/1 lb 2 oz pumpkin or butternut
  squash, peeled and seeded
3 tbsp olive oil
1 onion, finely chopped
2 garlic cloves, crushed
4–6 tbsp chopped fresh parsley

pinch of freshly grated nutmeg
about 250 ml/9 fl oz/1^1/$_4$ cups
  chicken or vegetable stock
115 g/4 oz Parma ham (prosciutto)
250 g/9 oz dried tagliatelle

150 ml/^{1}/$_4$ pint/^{5}/$_8$ cup double
  (heavy) cream
salt and pepper
freshly grated Parmesan cheese,
  to serve

1 Cut the pumpkin or butternut squash in half and scoop out the seeds with a spoon. Cut the pumpkin or squash into 1 cm/½ inch dice.

2 Heat 2 tbsp of the olive oil in a large saucepan. Add the onion and garlic and fry over a low heat for about 3 minutes, until soft. Add half the parsley and fry for 1 minute.

3 Add the pumpkin or squash pieces and cook for 2–3 minutes. Season to taste with salt, pepper and nutmeg.

4 Add half the stock to the pan, bring to the boil, cover and simmer for about 10 minutes, or until the pumpkin or squash is tender. Add more stock if the pumpkin or squash is becoming dry and looks as if it might burn.

5 Add the Parma ham (prosciutto) to the pan and cook, stirring frequently, for a further 2 minutes.

6 Meanwhile, bring a large saucepan of lightly salted water to the boil. Add the tagliatelle and the remaining oil and cook for 12 minutes, until tender, but still firm to the bite. Drain the pasta and transfer to a warm serving dish.

7 Stir the cream into the pumpkin and ham mixture and heat through. Spoon over the pasta, sprinkle over the remaining parsley and serve. Hand the grated Parmesan separately.

Aubergine (Eggplant) Cake

Layers of toasty-brown aubergine (eggplant), meat sauce and cheese-flavoured pasta make this a popular family supper dish.

Serves 4

INGREDIENTS

1 aubergine (eggplant), thinly sliced
5 tbsp olive oil
250 g/8 oz/2 cups dried fusilli
600 ml/1 pint/2½ cups Béchamel
  sauce (see page 166)
90 g/3 oz/¾ cup grated
  Cheddar cheese
butter, for greasing

25 g/1 oz/⅓ cup freshly grated
  Parmesan cheese
salt and pepper

LAMB SAUCE:
2 tbsp olive oil
1 large onion, sliced
2 celery sticks (stalks), thinly sliced

450 g/1 lb minced (ground) lamb
3 tbsp tomato purée (paste)
150 g/5½ oz bottled sun-dried
  tomatoes, drained and chopped
1 tsp dried oregano
1 tbsp red wine vinegar
150 ml/¼ pint/⅝ cup chicken stock
salt and pepper

1 Put the aubergine (eggplant) slices in a colander, sprinkle with salt and set aside for 45 minutes.

2 To make the lamb sauce, heat the oil in a pan. Fry the onion and celery for 3–4 minutes. Add the lamb and fry, stirring frequently, until browned. Stir in the remaining sauce ingredients, bring to the boil and cook for 20 minutes.

3 Rinse the aubergine (eggplant) slices, drain and pat dry. Heat 4 tbsp of the oil in a frying pan (skillet). Fry the aubergine (eggplant) slices for about 4 minutes on each side. Remove from the pan and drain well.

4 Bring a large pan of lightly salted water to the boil. Add the fusilli and the remaining oil and cook until almost tender, but still firm to the bite. Drain well.

5 Gently heat the Béchamel Sauce, stirring constantly. Stir in the Cheddar cheese. Stir half of the cheese sauce into the fusilli.

6 Make layers of fusilli, lamb sauce and aubergine (eggplant) slices in a greased dish. Spread the remaining cheese sauce over the top. Sprinkle over the Parmesan and bake in a preheated oven at 190°C/375°F/Gas 5 for 25 minutes. Serve hot or cold.

Wholemeal (Whole-wheat) Spaghetti with Suprêmes of Chicken Nell Gwyn

The refreshing combination of chicken and orange sauce
makes this a perfect dish for a warm summer evening.

Serves 4

INGREDIENTS

25 ml/1 fl oz/^{1}/8 cup rapeseed oil
3 tbsp olive oil
4 x 225 g/8 oz chicken suprêmes
150 ml/^{1}/4 pint/^{5}/8 cup
orange brandy
15 g/^{1}/2 oz/2 tbsp plain
(all purpose) flour
150 ml/^{1}/4 pint/^{5}/8 cup freshly
squeezed orange juice

25 g/1 oz courgette (zucchini), cut
into matchstick strips
25 g/1 oz red (bell) pepper, cut into
matchstick strips
25 g/1 oz leek, finely shredded
400 g/14 oz dried wholemeal (whole-
wheat) spaghetti
3 large oranges, peeled and cut
into segments

rind of 1 orange, cut into very
fine strips
2 tbsp chopped fresh tarragon
150 ml/^{1}/4 pint/^{5}/8 cup fromage frais
or ricotta cheese
salt and pepper
fresh tarragon leaves, to garnish

1 Heat the rapeseed oil and 1 tbsp of the olive oil in a frying pan (skillet). Add the chicken and cook quickly until golden brown. Add the orange brandy and cook for 3 minutes. Sprinkle over the flour and cook for 2 minutes.

2 Lower the heat and add the orange juice, courgette (zucchini), (bell) pepper and leek and season. Simmer for 5 minutes until the sauce has thickened.

3 Meanwhile, bring a pan of salted water to the boil. Add the spaghetti and 1 tbsp of the olive oil and cook for 10 minutes. Drain, transfer to a serving dish and drizzle over the remaining oil.

4 Add half the orange segments, half the orange rind, the tarragon and fromage frais or ricotta cheese to the sauce in the pan and cook for 3 minutes.

5 Place the chicken on top of the pasta, pour over a little sauce, garnish with orange segments, rind and tarragon. Serve immediately.

Chicken & Wild Mushroom Lasagne

You can use your favourite mushrooms, such as chanterelles or oyster mushrooms, for this delicately flavoured dish.

Serves 4

INGREDIENTS

butter, for greasing
14 sheets pre-cooked lasagne
850 ml/1$\frac{1}{2}$ pints/3$\frac{3}{4}$ cups Béchamel
    Sauce (see page 166)
75 g/3 oz/1 cup grated
    Parmesan cheese

CHICKEN & WILD MUSHROOM
    SAUCE:
2 tbsp olive oil
2 garlic cloves, crushed
1 large onion, finely chopped
225 g/8 oz wild mushrooms, sliced
300 g/10$\frac{1}{2}$ oz/2$\frac{1}{2}$ cups minced
    (ground) chicken

80 g/3 oz chicken livers,
    finely chopped
115 g/4 oz Parma ham
    (prosciutto), diced
150 ml/$\frac{1}{4}$ pint/$\frac{5}{8}$ cup Marsala
285g/10 oz can chopped tomatoes
1 tbsp chopped fresh basil leaves
2 tbsp tomato purée (paste)
salt and pepper

1 To make the chicken and wild mushroom sauce, heat the olive oil in a large saucepan. Add the garlic, onion and mushrooms and cook, stirring frequently, for 6 minutes.

2 Add the minced (ground) chicken, chicken livers and Parma ham (prosciutto) and cook over a low heat for 12 minutes, until the meat has browned.

3 Stir the Marsala, tomatoes, basil and tomato purée (paste) into the mixture in the pan and cook for 4 minutes. Season to taste with salt and pepper, cover and simmer for 30 minutes. Uncover the pan, stir and simmer for a further 15 minutes.

4 Lightly grease an ovenproof dish with butter. Arrange sheets of lasagne over the base of the dish, spoon over a layer of chicken and wild mushroom sauce, then spoon over a layer of Béchamel Sauce. Place another layer of lasagne on top and repeat the process twice, finishing with a layer of Béchamel Sauce. Sprinkle over the grated cheese and bake in a preheated oven at 190°C/375°F/Gas 5 for 35 minutes until golden brown and bubbling. Serve immediately.

Tagliatelle with Chicken Sauce

Spinach ribbon noodles with a rich tomato sauce and topped
with creamy chicken make a very appetizing dish.

Serves 4

INGREDIENTS

250 g/9 oz fresh green tagliatelle
1 tbsp olive oil
salt
fresh basil leaves, to garnish

TOMATO SAUCE:
2 tbsp olive oil
1 small onion, chopped

1 garlic clove, chopped
400 g/14 oz can chopped tomatoes
2 tbsp chopped fresh parsley
1 tsp dried oregano
2 bay leaves
2 tbsp tomato purée (paste)
1 tsp sugar
salt and pepper

CHICKEN SAUCE:
60 g/2 oz/4 tbsp unsalted butter
400 g/14 oz boned chicken breasts,
   skinned and cut into thin strips
90 g/3 oz/$^3/_4$ cup blanched almonds
300 ml/$^1/_2$ pint/1$^1/_4$ cups double
   (heavy) cream
salt and pepper

1 To make the tomato sauce, heat the oil in a pan over a medium heat. Add the onion and fry until translucent. Add the garlic and fry for 1 minute. Stir in the garlic, tomatoes, parsley, oregano, bay leaves, tomato purée (paste), sugar and salt and pepper to taste, bring to the boil and simmer, uncovered, for 15–20 minutes, until reduced by half. Remove the pan from the heat and discard the bay leaves.

2 To make the chicken sauce, melt the butter in a frying pan (skillet) over a medium heat. Add the chicken and almonds and stir-fry for 5–6 minutes, until the chicken is cooked through.

3 Meanwhile, bring the cream to the boil in a small pan over a low heat and boil for about 10 minutes, until reduced by almost half. Pour the cream over the chicken and almonds, stir and season to taste with salt and pepper. Set aside and keep warm.

4 Bring a large pan of lightly salted water to the boil. Add the tagliatelle and olive oil and cook until tender, but still firm to the bite. Drain and transfer to a warm serving dish. Spoon over the tomato sauce and arrange the chicken sauce down the centre. Garnish with the basil leaves and serve immediately.

Mustard Baked Chicken with Pasta Shells

Chicken pieces are cooked in a succulent, mild mustard sauce, then coated in poppy seeds and served on a bed of fresh pasta shells.

Serves 4

INGREDIENTS

8 chicken pieces
  (about 115 g/4 oz each)
60g/2 oz/4 tbsp butter, melted
4 tbsp mild mustard (see Cook's Tip)

2 tbsp lemon juice
1 tbsp brown sugar
1 tsp paprika
3 tbsp poppy seeds

400 g/14 oz fresh pasta shells
1 tbsp olive oil
salt and pepper

1 Arrange the chicken pieces, smooth side down, in a single layer in a large ovenproof dish.

2 Mix together the butter, mustard, lemon juice, sugar and paprika in a bowl and season to taste with salt and pepper. Brush the mixture over the upper surfaces of the chicken pieces and bake in a preheated oven at 200°C/400°F/Gas 6 for 15 minutes.

3 Remove the dish from the oven and carefully turn over the chicken pieces. Coat the upper surfaces of the chicken with the remaining mustard mixture, sprinkle the chicken pieces with poppy seeds and return to the oven for a further 15 minutes.

4 Meanwhile, bring a large pan of lightly salted water to the boil. Add the pasta shells and olive oil and cook until tender, but still firm to the bite.

5 Drain the pasta and arrange on a warmed serving dish. Top with the chicken, pour over the sauce and serve immediately.

COOK'S TIP

Dijon is the type of mustard most often used in cooking, as it has a clean and only mildly spicy flavour. German mustard has a sweet-sour taste, with Bavarian mustard being slightly sweeter. American mustard is mild and sweet.

Tortellini

Tortellini were said to have been created in the image of the goddess Venus's navel.
Whatever the story, these delicate filled pasta swirls offer a delicious blend of Italian flavours.

Serves 4

INGREDIENTS

115 g/4 oz boned chicken breast,
  skinned
60 g/2 oz Parma ham (prosciutto)
40 g/1¹/₂ oz cooked spinach,
  well drained
1 tbsp finely chopped onion
2 tbsp freshly grated
  Parmesan cheese

pinch of ground allspice
1 egg, beaten
450 g/1 lb Basic Pasta Dough (see
  page 4)
salt and pepper
2 tbsp chopped fresh parsley,
  to garnish

SAUCE:
300 ml/¹/₂ pint/1¹/₄ cups single
  (light) cream
2 garlic cloves, crushed
115 g/4 oz button mushrooms,
  thinly sliced
4 tbsp freshly grated Parmesan
  cheese

1 Bring a pan of seasoned water to the boil. Add the chicken and poach for about 10 minutes. Cool slightly, then put in a food processor, with the Parma ham (prosciutto), spinach and onion and process until finely chopped. Stir in the Parmesan cheese, allspice and egg and season to taste.

2 Thinly roll out the pasta dough and cut into 4–5 cm/ 1¹/₂–2 inch rounds.

3 Place ¹/₂ tsp of the filling in the centre of each round. Fold the pieces in half and press the edges to seal. Then wrap each piece around your index finger, cross over the ends and curl the rest of the dough backwards to make a navel shape. Re-roll the trimmings and repeat until all the dough is used up.

4 Bring a pan of salted water to the boil. Add the tortellini, in

batches, bring back to the boil and cook for 5 minutes. Drain and transfer to a serving dish.

5 To make the sauce, bring the cream and garlic to the boil in a small pan, then simmer for 3 minutes. Add the mushrooms and half the cheese, season and simmer for 2–3 minutes. Pour the sauce over the tortellini. Sprinkle over the remaining Parmesan cheese, garnish with the parsley and serve.

Chicken Suprêmes Filled with Tiger Prawns (Shrimp) on a Bed of Pasta

These mouth-watering mini-parcels of chicken and prawns (shrimp) will delight your guests.

Serves 4

INGREDIENTS

60 g/2 oz/4 tbsp butter, plus extra
   for greasing
4 x 200 g/7 oz chicken
   suprêmes, trimmed
115 g/4 oz large spinach leaves,
   trimmed and blanched in hot
   salted water

4 slices of Parma ham (prosciutto)
12–16 raw tiger prawns (shrimp),
   shelled and deveined
450g/1 lb dried tagliatelle
1 tbsp olive oil
3 leeks, shredded
1 large carrot, grated

150 ml/^{1}/4 pint/^{5}/8 cup
   thick mayonnaise
2 large cooked beetroot (beet)
salt

1 Grease 4 large pieces of foil and set aside. Place each suprême between 2 pieces of baking parchment and pound with a rolling pin to flatten.

2 Divide half of the spinach between the suprêmes, add a slice of ham to each and top with more spinach. Place 3–4 prawns (shrimp) on top of the spinach. Fold the pointed end of the suprême over the prawns (shrimp), then fold over again to form a parcel. Wrap in foil, place on a baking (cookie) sheet and bake in a preheated oven at 200°C/400°F/Gas 6 for 20 minutes.

3 Bring a pan of salted water to the boil. Add the pasta and oil and cook until tender. Drain and transfer to a serving dish.

4 Melt the butter in a frying pan (skillet). Fry the leeks and carrots for 3 minutes. Transfer the vegetables to the centre of the pasta.

5 Work the mayonnaise and 1 beetroot (beet) in a food processor or blender until smooth. Rub through a strainer and pour around the pasta and vegetables.

6 Cut the remaining beetroot (beet) into diamond shapes and place them neatly around the mayonnaise. Remove the foil from the chicken and, using a sharp knife, cut the suprêmes into thin slices. Arrange the slices on top of the vegetables and pasta, and serve.

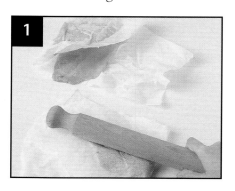

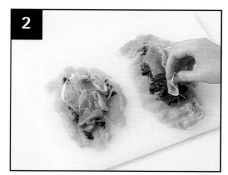

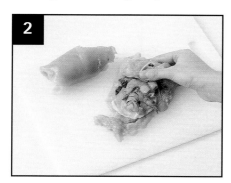

Chicken & Lobster on a Bed of Penne

While this is certainly a treat to get the taste buds tingling, it is not as extravagant as it sounds.

Serves 6

INGREDIENTS

butter, for greasing
6 chicken breasts
450 g/1 lb dried penne rigate
6 tbsp extra virgin olive oil
90 g/3 oz/1 cup freshly grated
    Parmesan cheese

salt

FILLING:
115 g/4 oz lobster meat, chopped
2 shallots, very finely chopped
2 figs, chopped

1 tbsp Marsala
2 tbsp breadcrumbs
1 large egg, beaten
salt and pepper

1 Grease 6 pieces of foil large enough to enclose each chicken breast and lightly grease a baking (cookie) sheet.

2 Place all of the filling ingredients into a mixing bowl and blend together thoroughly with a spoon.

3 Cut a pocket in each chicken breast with a sharp knife and fill with the lobster mixture. Wrap each chicken breast in foil, place the parcels on the greased baking

(cookie) sheet and bake in a preheated oven at 200°C/400°F/ Gas 6 for 30 minutes.

4 Meanwhile, bring a large pan of lightly salted water to the boil. Add the pasta and 1 tbsp of the olive oil and cook for about 10 minutes, or until tender but still firm to the bite. Drain the pasta thoroughly and transfer to a large serving plate. Sprinkle over the remaining olive oil and the grated Parmesan cheese, set aside and keep warm.

5 Carefully remove the foil from around the chicken breasts. Slice the breasts very thinly, arrange over the pasta and serve immediately.

COOK'S TIP

The cut of chicken known as suprême consists of the breast and wing. It is always skinned.

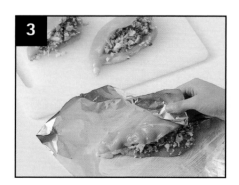

Chicken with Green Olives & Pasta

Olives are a popular flavouring for poultry and game in the
Apulia region of Italy, where this recipe originates.

Serves 4

INGREDIENTS

3 tbsp olive oil
25 g/1 oz/2 tbsp butter
4 chicken breasts, part boned
1 large onion, finely chopped
2 garlic cloves, crushed
2 red, yellow or green (bell) peppers,
 cored, seeded and cut into
 large pieces

250 g/9 oz button mushrooms, sliced
 or quartered
175 g/6 oz tomatoes, skinned
 and halved
150 ml/¼ pint/⅝ cup dry
 white wine
175 g/6 oz/1½ cups stoned (pitted)
 green olives

4–6 tbsp double (heavy) cream
400 g/14 oz dried pasta
salt and pepper
chopped flat leaf parsley, to garnish

1 Heat 2 tbsp of the oil and the butter in a frying pan (skillet). Add the chicken breasts and fry until golden brown all over. Remove the chicken from the pan.

2 Add the onion and garlic to the pan and fry over a medium heat until beginning to soften. Add the (bell) peppers and mushrooms and cook for 2–3 minutes. Add the tomatoes and season to taste with salt and

pepper. Transfer the vegetables to a casserole and arrange the chicken on top.

3 Add the wine to the pan and bring to the boil. Pour the wine over the chicken. Cover and cook in a preheated oven at 180°C/ 350°F/Gas 4 for 50 minutes.

4 Add the olives to the casserole and mix in. Pour in the cream, cover and return to the oven for 10–20 minutes.

5 Meanwhile, bring a large pan of lightly salted water to the boil. Add the pasta and the remaining oil and cook until tender, but still firm to the bite. Drain the pasta well and transfer to a serving dish.

6 Arrange the chicken on top of the pasta, spoon over the sauce, garnish with the parsley and serve immediately. Alternatively, place the pasta in a large serving bowl and serve separately.

Sliced Breast of Duckling with Linguine

A raspberry and honey sauce superbly counterbalances the richness of the duckling.

Serves 4

INGREDIENTS

4 x 275 g/10$^{1}/_{2}$ oz boned breasts
  of duckling
25 g/1 oz/2 tbsp butter
50 g/2 oz/$^{3}/_{8}$ cup finely
  chopped carrots
50 g/2 oz/4 tbsp finely
  chopped shallots
1 tbsp lemon juice

150 ml/$^{1}/_{4}$ pint/$^{5}/_{8}$ cup meat stock
4 tbsp clear honey
115 g/4 oz/$^{3}/_{4}$ cup fresh or thawed
  frozen raspberries
25 g/1 oz/$^{1}/_{4}$ cup plain (all
  purpose) flour
1 tbsp Worcestershire sauce
400 g/14 oz fresh linguine

1 tbsp olive oil
salt and pepper

TO GARNISH:
fresh raspberries
fresh sprig of flat-leaf parsley

1 Trim and score the duck breasts with a sharp knife and season well all over. Melt the butter in a frying pan (skillet), add the duck breasts and fry all over until lightly coloured.

2 Add the carrots, shallots, lemon juice and half the meat stock and simmer over a low heat for 1 minute. Stir in half the honey and half the raspberries. Sprinkle over half the flour and cook, stirring constantly for

3 minutes. Season with pepper and add the Worcestershire sauce.

3 Stir in the remaining stock and cook for 1 minute. Stir in the remaining honey and remaining raspberries and sprinkle over the remaining flour. Cook for a further 3 minutes.

4 Remove the duck breasts from the pan, but leave the sauce to continue simmering over a very low heat.

5 Meanwhile, bring a large saucepan of lightly salted water to the boil. Add the linguine and olive oil and cook until tender, but still firm to the bite. Drain and divide between 4 individual plates.

6 Slice the duck breast lengthways into 5 mm/ $^{1}/_{4}$ inch thick pieces. Pour a little sauce over the pasta and arrange the sliced duck in a fan shape on top of it. Garnish with raspberries and flat-leaf parsley and serve.

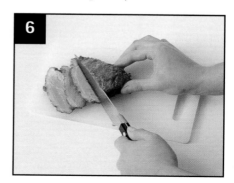

Rigatoni & Pesto Baked Partridge

Partridge has a more delicate flavour than many game birds and this subtle sauce perfectly complements it.

Serves 4

INGREDIENTS

8 partridge pieces
  (about 115 g/4 oz each)
60 g/2 oz/4 tbsp butter, melted
4 tbsp Dijon mustard

2 tbsp lime juice
1 tbsp brown sugar
6 tbsp Pesto Sauce (see page 12)
450 g/1 lb dried rigatoni

1 tbsp olive oil
115 g/4 oz/1$\frac{1}{3}$ cups freshly grated
  Parmesan cheese
salt and pepper

1 Arrange the partridge pieces, smooth side down, in a single layer in a large, ovenproof dish.

2 Mix together the butter, Dijon mustard, lime juice and brown sugar in a bowl. Season to taste with salt and pepper. Brush this mixture over the uppermost surfaces of the partridge pieces and bake in a preheated oven at 200°C/400°F/Gas 6 for 15 minutes.

3 Remove the dish from the oven and coat the partridge pieces with 3 tbsp of the Pesto Sauce. Return to the oven and bake for a further 12 minutes.

4 Remove the dish from the oven and carefully turn over the partridge pieces. Coat the top of the partridges with the remaining mustard mixture and return to the oven for a further 10 minutes.

5 Meanwhile, bring a large saucepan of lightly salted water to the boil. Add the rigatoni and olive oil and cook for about 10 minutes, until tender, but still firm to the bite. Drain and transfer to a large serving dish. Toss the pasta with the remaining Pesto Sauce and the Parmesan cheese.

6 Arrange the pieces of partridge on the serving dish with the rigatoni, pour over the cooking juices and serve immediately.

VARIATION

You could also prepare young pheasant in the same way.

Breast of Pheasant Lasagne with Baby Onions & Green Peas

This scrumptious and unusual baked lasagne is virtually a meal in itself.

Serves 4

INGREDIENTS

butter, for greasing
14 sheets pre-cooked lasagne
850 ml/1¹/₃ pints/3³/₄ cups Béchamel
  Sauce (see page 166)
75 g/3 oz/³/₄ cup grated
  mozzarella cheese

FILLING:
225 g/8 oz pork fat, diced
60 g/2 oz/2 tbsp butter
16 small onions
8 large pheasant breasts, thinly sliced

25 g/1 oz/¹/₄ cup plain
  (all purpose) flour
600 ml/1 pint/2¹/₂ cups chicken stock
bouquet garni
450 g/1 lb fresh peas, shelled
salt and pepper

1 To make the filling, put the pork fat into a pan of boiling, salted water and simmer for 3 minutes, then drain and pat dry.

2 Melt the butter in a large frying pan (skillet). Add the pork fat and onions and cook for 3 minutes, until lightly browned.

3 Remove the pork fat and onions from the pan and set aside. Add the slices of pheasant and cook over a low heat for

12 minutes, until browned all over. Transfer to an ovenproof dish.

4 Stir the flour into the pan and cook until just brown, then blend in the stock. Pour over the pheasant, add the bouquet garni and cook in a preheated oven at 200°C/400°F/Gas 6 for 5 minutes.

5 Remove the bouquet garni. Add the onions, pork fat and peas and return to the oven for 10 minutes.

6 Put the pheasant breasts and pork in a food processor and mince (grind) finely.

7 Lower the oven temperature to 190°C/375°F/Gas 5. Lightly grease an ovenproof dish with butter. Make layers of lasagne, pheasant sauce and Béchamel Sauce in the dish, ending with Béchamel sauce. Sprinkle over the cheese and bake in the oven for 30 minutes. Serve surrounded by the peas and onions.

Fish & Seafood

Pasta is a natural partner for fish and seafood. Both are cooked quickly to preserve their flavour and texture, they are packed full of nutritional goodness and the varieties available are almost infinite. The superb recipes in this chapter demonstrate the full range of these qualities. For a quick, easy and satisfying supper, try Spaghetti al Tonno, Casserole of Fusilli & Smoked Haddock with Egg Sauce, Seafood Lasagne or Macaroni and Prawn (Shrimp) Bake. More unusual and sophisticated dishes include Sea Bass with Olive Sauce on a Bed of Macaroni, Poached Salmon Steaks with Penne, Farfallini Buttered Lobster and Baked Scallops with Pasta in Shells. There are dishes to suit all tastes – freshwater and sea fish, shellfish and other seafood – and to suit all pockets. All are easy to make; the only problem is choosing which one to cook next.

Cannelloni Filetti di Sogliola

This is a lighter dish than the better-known cannelloni stuffed with minced beef.

Serves 6

INGREDIENTS

12 small fillets of sole
(about 115 g/4 oz each)
150 ml/¼ pint/⅝ cup red wine
90 g/3 oz/6 tbsp butter
115 g/4 oz/3⅞ cups sliced
button mushrooms
4 shallots, finely chopped

115 g/4 oz tomatoes, chopped
2 tbsp tomato purée (paste)
60 g/2 oz/½ cup plain (all purpose)
flour, sifted
150 ml/¼ pint/⅝ cup of
warm milk
2 tbsp double (heavy) cream

6 dried cannelloni tubes
175 g/6 oz cooked, peeled prawns
(shrimp), preferably freshwater
salt and pepper
1 fresh fennel sprig, to garnish

1 Brush the fillets with a little wine, season with salt and pepper and roll them up, skin side inwards. Secure with a skewer or cocktail stick (toothpick).

2 Arrange the fish rolls in a single layer in a large frying pan (skillet), add the remaining red wine and poach for about 4 minutes. Remove from the pan and reserve the cooking liquid.

3 Melt the butter in another pan. Fry the mushrooms and shallots for 2 minutes, then add the tomatoes and tomato purée (paste). Season the flour and stir it into the pan. Stir in the reserved cooking liquid and half the milk. Cook over a low heat, stirring, for 4 minutes. Remove from the heat and stir in the cream.

4 Bring a large saucepan of lightly salted water to the boil. Add the cannelloni and cook for about 8 minutes, until tender but still firm to the bite. Drain and set aside to cool.

5 Remove the skewers or cocktail sticks (toothpicks) from the fish rolls. Put 2 sole fillets into each cannelloni tube with 2–3 prawns (shrimp) and a little red wine sauce. Arrange the cannelloni in an ovenproof dish, pour over the sauce and bake in a preheated oven at 200°C/400°F/ Gas 6 for 20 minutes.

6 Serve the cannelloni with the red wine sauce, garnished with the remaining prawns (shrimp) and a sprig of fennel.

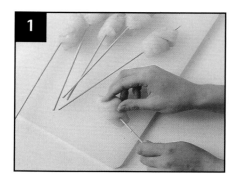

Sea Bass with Olive Sauce on a Bed of Macaroni

A favourite fish for chefs, the delicious sea bass is now becoming increasingly common in supermarkets and fish stores for family meals.

Serves 4

INGREDIENTS

450 g/1 lb dried macaroni
1 tbsp olive oil
8 x 115 g/4 oz sea bass medallions

TO GARNISH:
lemon slices
shredded leek
shredded carrot

SAUCE:
25 g/1 oz/2 tbsp butter
4 shallots, chopped
2 tbsp capers
175 g/6 oz/1$^{1}/_{2}$ cups stoned (pitted)
  green olives, chopped
4 tbsp balsamic vinegar
300 ml/$^{1}/_{2}$ pint/1$^{1}/_{4}$ cups fish stock

300 ml/$^{1}/_{2}$ pint/1$^{1}/_{4}$ cups double
  (heavy) cream
juice of 1 lemon
salt and pepper

1 To make the sauce, melt the butter in a frying pan (skillet). Add the shallots and cook over a low heat for 4 minutes. Add the capers and olives and cook for a further 3 minutes.

2 Stir in the balsamic vinegar and fish stock, bring to the boil and reduce by half. Add the cream, stirring, and reduce again by half. Season to taste with salt and pepper and stir in the lemon juice. Remove the pan from the heat, set aside and keep warm.

3 Bring a large saucepan of lightly salted water to the boil. Add the pasta and olive oil and cook for about 12 minutes, until tender but still firm to the bite.

4 Meanwhile, lightly grill (broil) the sea bass medallions for 3–4 minutes on each side, until cooked through, but still moist and delicate.

5 Drain the pasta thoroughly and transfer to large individual serving dishes. Top the pasta with the fish medallions and pour over the olive sauce. Garnish with lemon slices, shredded leek and shredded carrot and serve immediately.

Spaghetti alla Bucaniera

*Brill was once known as poor man's turbot, an unfair description
as it is a delicately flavoured and delicious fish in its own right.*

Serves 4

INGREDIENTS

90 g/3 oz/³/4 cup plain
  (all purpose) flour
450 g/1 lb brill or sole fillets, skinned
  and chopped
450 g/1 lb hake fillets, skinned
  and chopped
90 g/3 oz/6 tbsp butter
4 shallots, finely chopped

2 garlic cloves, crushed
1 carrot, diced
1 leek, finely chopped
300 ml/¹/2 pint/1¹/4 cups dry
  (hard) cider
300 ml/¹/2 pint/1¹/4 cups medium
  sweet cider
2 tsp anchovy essence (extract)

1 tbsp tarragon vinegar
450 g/1 lb dried spaghetti
1 tbsp olive oil
salt and pepper
chopped fresh parsley, to garnish
crusty brown bread, to serve

1 Season the flour with salt and
pepper. Sprinkle 25 g/1 oz/¹/4
cup of the seasoned flour on to a
shallow plate. Press the fish pieces
into the seasoned flour to coat
thoroughly.

2 Melt the butter in a
flameproof casserole. Add the
fish fillets, shallots, garlic, carrot
and leek and cook over a low heat,
stirring frequently, for about
10 minutes.

3 Sprinkle over the remaining
seasoned flour and cook,
stirring constantly, for 2 minutes.
Gradually stir in the cider, anchovy
essence (extract) and tarragon
vinegar. Bring to the boil and
simmer over a low heat for
35 minutes. Alternatively, bake
in a preheated oven at 180°C/
350°F/Gas 4 for 30 minutes.

4 About 15 minutes before the
end of the cooking time,

bring a large pan of lightly salted
water to the boil. Add the spaghetti
and olive oil and cook for about
12 minutes, until tender but still
firm to the bite. Drain the pasta
thoroughly and transfer to a large
serving dish.

5 Arrange the fish on top of the
spaghetti and pour over the
sauce. Garnish with chopped
parsley and serve immediately with
warm, crusty brown bread.

Steamed Pasta Pudding

A tasty mixture of creamy fish and pasta cooked in a bowl, unmoulded and drizzled with tomato sauce presents macaroni in a new guise.

Serves 4

INGREDIENTS

115 g/4 oz/1 cup dried short-cut
 macaroni or other short pasta
1 tbsp olive oil
15 g/^{1}/$_2$ oz/1 tbsp butter, pus extra
 for greasing
450 g/1 lb white fish fillets, such as
 cod or haddock

2–3 fresh parsley sprigs
6 black peppercorns
125 ml/4 fl oz/^{1}/$_2$ cup double
 (heavy) cream
2 eggs, separated
2 tbsp chopped fresh dill or parsley
pinch of freshly grated nutmeg

60 g/2 oz/^{2}/$_3$ cup freshly grated
 Parmesan cheese
salt and pepper
fresh dill or parsley sprigs, to garnish
tomato sauce (see page 54), to serve

1 Bring a pan of salted water to the boil. Add the pasta and olive oil and cook until tender, but still firm to the bite. Drain the pasta, return to the pan, add the butter, cover and keep warm.

2 Place the fish in a frying pan (skillet). Add the parsley sprigs, peppercorns and enough water to cover. Bring to the boil, cover and simmer for 10 minutes. Lift out the fish and set aside to cool. Reserve the cooking liquid.

3 Skin the fish and cut into bite-size pieces. Put the pasta in a bowl. Mix the cream, egg yolks, chopped dill or parsley, nutmeg and cheese, pour into the pasta and mix. Spoon in the fish without breaking it. Add enough of the reserved cooking liquid to make a moist, but firm mixture. Whisk the egg whites until stiff, then fold them into the mixture.

4 Grease a heatproof bowl and spoon in the fish mixture to

within 4 cm/1^1/$_2$ inches of the rim. Cover with greased greaseproof (baking) paper and foil and tie securely with string.

5 Stand the bowl on a trivet in a saucepan. Add boiling water to reach halfway up the sides. Cover and steam for 1^1/$_2$ hours.

6 Invert the pudding on to a serving plate. Pour over a little tomato sauce. Garnish and serve with the remaining tomato sauce.

Red Mullet Fillets with Orecchiette, Amaretto & Orange Sauce

This succulent fish and pasta dish is ideal for serving on a warm, summer's evening – preferably al fresco.

Serves 4

INGREDIENTS

90 g/3 oz/3³/₄ cup plain
  (all purpose) flour
8 red mullet fillets
25 g/1 oz/2 tbsp butter
150 ml/¹/₄ pint/⁵/₈ cup fish stock
1 tbsp crushed almonds
1 tsp pink peppercorns

1 orange, peeled and cut
  into segments
1 tbsp orange liqueur
grated rind of 1 orange
450 g/1 lb dried orecchiette
1 tbsp olive oil
150 ml/¹/₄ pint/⁵/₈ cup double
  (heavy) cream

4 tbsp amaretto
salt and pepper

TO GARNISH:
2 tbsp snipped fresh chives
1 tbsp toasted almonds

1 Season the flour with salt and pepper and sprinkle into a shallow bowl. Press the fish fillets into the flour to coat. Melt the butter in a frying pan (skillet). Add the fish and fry over a low heat for 3 minutes, until browned.

2 Add the fish stock to the pan and cook for 4 minutes. Carefully remove the fish, cover with foil and keep warm.

3 Add the almonds, pink peppercorns, half the orange, the orange liqueur and orange rind to the pan. Simmer until the liquid has reduced by half.

4 Meanwhile, bring a large saucepan of lightly salted water to the boil. Add the orecchiette and olive oil and cook for 15 minutes, until tender but still firm to the bite.

5 Meanwhile, season the sauce with salt and pepper and stir in the cream and amaretto. Cook for 2 minutes. Return the fish to the pan to coat with the sauce.

6 Drain the pasta and transfer to a serving dish. Top with the fish fillets and their sauce. Garnish with the remaining orange segments, the chives and toasted almonds. Serve immediately.

Vermicelli with Fillets of Red Mullet

*This simple recipe perfectly complements
the sweet flavour and delicate texture of the fish.*

Serves 4

INGREDIENTS

1 kg/2$\frac{1}{4}$ lb red mullet fillets
300 ml/$\frac{1}{2}$ pint/1$\frac{1}{4}$ cups dry white
  wine
4 shallots, finely chopped
1 garlic clove, crushed
3 tbsp finely chopped mixed
  fresh herbs

finely grated rind and juice of
  1 lemon
pinch of freshly grated nutmeg
3 anchovy fillets, roughly chopped
2 tbsp double (heavy) cream
1 tsp cornflour (cornstarch)
450 g/1 lb dried vermicelli

1 tbsp olive oil
salt and pepper

TO GARNISH:
1 fresh mint sprig
lemon slices
lemon rind

1 Put the red mullet fillets in a large casserole. Pour over the wine and add the shallots, garlic, chopped herbs, lemon rind and juice, nutmeg and anchovies. Season to taste with salt and pepper. Cover and bake in a preheated oven at 180°C/350°F/ Gas 4 for 35 minutes.

2 Carefully transfer the mullet to a warm dish. Set aside and keep warm while you prepare the sauce and pasta.

3 Pour the cooking liquid into a pan and bring to the boil. Simmer for 25 minutes, until reduced by half. Mix together the cream and cornflour (cornstarch) and stir into the sauce to thicken.

4 Meanwhile, bring a large pan of lightly salted water to the boil. Add the vermicelli and olive oil and cook for 8–10 minutes, until tender, but still firm to the bite. Drain the pasta and transfer to a warm serving dish.

5 Arrange the red mullet fillets on top of the vermicelli and pour over the sauce. Garnish with a fresh mint sprig, slices of lemon and strips of lemon rind and serve immediately.

COOK'S TIP

The best red mullet is sometimes called golden mullet, although it is bright red in colour.

Spaghetti al Tonno

The classic Italian combination of pasta and tuna is enhanced in this recipe with a delicious parsley sauce.

Serves 4

INGREDIENTS

200 g/7 oz can tuna, drained
60 g/2 oz can anchovies, drained
250 ml/9 fl oz/1⅛ cups olive oil

60 g/2 oz/1 cup roughly chopped flat leaf parsley
150 ml/¼ pint/⅝ cup crème fraîche
450 g/1 lb dried spaghetti

25 g/1 oz/2 tbsp butter
salt and pepper
black olives, to garnish
crusty bread, to serve

1 Remove any bones from the tuna. Put the tuna into a food processor or blender, together with the anchovies, 225 ml/8 fl oz/1 cup of the olive oil and the flat leaf parsley. Process until the sauce is smooth.

2 Spoon the crème fraîche into the food processor or blender and process again for a few seconds to blend thoroughly. Season to taste with salt and black pepper.

3 Bring a large pan of lightly salted water to the boil. Add the spaghetti and the remaining olive oil and cook until tender, but still firm to the bite.

4 Drain the spaghetti, return to the pan and place over a medium heat. Add the butter and toss well to coat. Spoon in the sauce and quickly toss into the spaghetti, using 2 forks.

5 Remove the pan from the heat and divide the spaghetti between 4 warm individual serving plates. Garnish with the olives and serve immediately with warm, crusty bread.

VARIATION

If liked, you could add 1–2 garlic cloves to the sauce, substitute 25 g/1 oz/½ cup chopped fresh basil for half the parsley and garnish with capers instead of black olives.

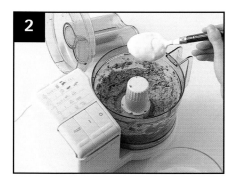

Casserole of Fusilli & Smoked Haddock with Egg Sauce

This quick, easy and inexpensive dish would be ideal for a mid-week family supper.

Serves 4

INGREDIENTS

25 g/1 oz/2 tbsp butter, plus extra
  for greasing
450 g/1 lb smoked haddock fillets,
  cut into 4 slices
600 ml/1 pint/2^1/$_2$ cups milk
25 g/1 oz/^{1}/$_4$ cup plain
  (all purpose) flour

pinch of freshly grated nutmeg
3 tbsp double (heavy) cream
1 tbsp chopped fresh parsley
2 eggs, hard boiled (hard cooked) and
  mashed to a pulp
450 g/1 lb/4 cups dried fusilli
1 tbsp lemon juice

salt and pepper
boiled new potatoes and beetroot
  (beet), to serve

1 Thoroughly grease a casserole with butter. Put the haddock in the casserole and pour over the milk. Bake in a preheated oven at 200°C/400°G/Gas 6 for about 15 minutes. Carefully pour the cooking liquid into a jug (pitcher) without breaking up the fish.

2 Melt the butter in a saucepan and stir in the flour. Gradually whisk in the reserved cooking liquid. Season to taste with salt, pepper and nutmeg. Stir in the cream, parsley and mashed egg and cook, stirring constantly, for 2 minutes.

3 Meanwhile, bring a large saucepan of lightly salted water to the boil. Add the fusilli and lemon juice and cook until tender, but still firm to the bite.

4 Drain the pasta and spoon or tip it over the fish. Top with the sauce and return the casserole to the oven for 10 minutes.

5 Serve the casserole with boiled new potatoes and beetroot (beet).

VARIATION

You can use any type of dried pasta for this casserole. Try penne, conchiglie or rigatoni.

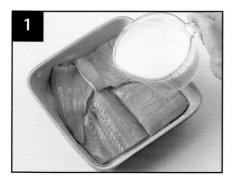

Ravioli of Lemon Sole & Haddock

This delicate-tasting dish is surprisingly satisfying for even the hungriest appetites.

Serves 4

INGREDIENTS

450 g/1 lb lemon sole fillets, skinned
450 g/1 lb haddock fillets, skinned
3 eggs beaten
450 g/1 lb cooked potato gnocchi
(see page 58)

175 g/6 oz/3 cups fresh breadcrumbs
50 ml/2 fl oz/^{1}/4 cup double
(heavy) cream
450 g/1 lb Basic Pasta Dough (see
page 4)

300 ml/^{1}/2 pint/1^1/4 cups Italian Red
Wine Sauce (see page 52)
60 g/2 oz/^{2}/3 cup freshly grated
Parmesan cheese
salt and pepper

1 Flake the lemon sole and haddock fillets with a fork and transfer the flesh to a large mixing bowl.

2 Mix the eggs, cooked potato gnocchi, breadcrumbs and cream in a bowl until thoroughly combined. Add the fish to the bowl containing the gnocchi and season the mixture to taste with salt and black pepper.

3 Roll out the pasta dough on to a lightly floured surface and cut out 7.5 cm/3 inch rounds using a plain cutter.

4 Place a spoonful of the fish stuffing on each round. Dampen the edges slightly and fold the pasta rounds over, pressing together to seal.

5 Bring a large saucepan of lightly salted water to the boil. Add the ravioli and cook for 15 minutes.

6 Drain the ravioli, using a slotted spoon, and transfer to a large serving dish. Pour over the Italian Red Wine Sauce, sprinkle over the Parmesan cheese and serve immediately.

COOK'S TIP

When making square ravioli, divide the dough into two. Wrap half in cling film (plastic wrap) and thinly roll out the other half. Cover with a clean, damp tea towel while you roll out the remaining dough. Spoon or pipe the filling at regular intervals and brush the spaces in between with water or beaten egg. Lift the second sheet of dough into position with a rolling pin and press firmly between the filling to seal and expel any air. Cut out the shapes with a ravioli cutter or a knife.

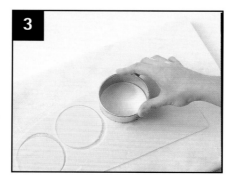

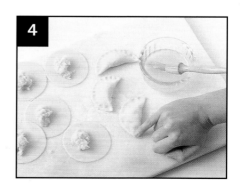

Poached Salmon Steaks with Penne

*Fresh salmon and pasta in a mouth-watering lemon and
watercress sauce – a wonderful summer evening treat.*

Serves 4

INGREDIENTS

4 x 275 g/10 oz fresh salmon steaks
60 g/2 oz/4 tbsp butter
175 ml/6 fl oz/³/₄ cup dry white wine
sea salt
8 peppercorns
fresh dill sprig
fresh tarragon sprig
1 lemon, sliced
450 g/1 lb dried penne

2 tbsp olive oil
lemon slices and fresh watercress,
 to garnish

LEMON & WATERCRESS SAUCE:
25 g/1 oz/2 tbsp butter
25 g/1 oz/¹/₄ cup plain (all purpose)
 flour
150 ml/¹/₄ pint/⁵/₈ cup warm milk

juice and finely grated rind of
 2 lemons
60 g/2 oz watercress, chopped
salt and pepper

1 Put the salmon in a large, non-stick pan. Add the butter, wine, a pinch of sea salt, the peppercorns, dill, tarragon and lemon. Cover, bring to the boil, and simmer for 10 minutes.

2 Using a fish slice, carefully remove the salmon. Strain and reserve the cooking liquid. Remove and discard the salmon skin and centre bones. Place on a warm dish, cover and keep warm.

3 Meanwhile, bring a saucepan of salted water to the boil. Add the penne and 1 tbsp of the oil and cook for 12 minutes, until tender but still firm to the bite. Drain and sprinkle over the remaining olive oil. Place on a warm serving dish, top with the salmon steaks and keep warm.

4 To make the sauce, melt the butter and stir in the flour for 2 minutes. Stir in the milk and

about 7 tbsp of the reserved cooking liquid. Add the lemon juice and rind and cook, stirring, for a further 10 minutes.

5 Add the watercress to the sauce, stir gently and season to taste with salt and pepper.

6 Pour the sauce over the salmon and penne, garnish with slices of lemon and fresh watercress and serve immediately.

Spaghetti with Smoked Salmon

*Made in moments, this is a luxurious dish
to astonish and delight unexpected guests.*

Serves 4

INGREDIENTS

450 g/1 lb dried buckwheat spaghetti
2 tbsp olive oil
90 g/3 oz/^{1}/$_2$ cup crumbled
   feta cheese
salt
fresh coriander (cilantro) or parsley
   leaves, to garnish

SAUCE:
300 ml/^{1}/$_2$ pint/1^1/$_4$ cups double
   (heavy) cream
150 ml/^{1}/$_4$ pint/^{5}/$_8$ cup whisky
   or brandy
125 g/4^1/$_2$ oz smoked salmon
pinch of cayenne pepper

black pepper
2 tbsp chopped fresh coriander
   (cilantro) or parsley

1 Bring a large pan of lightly salted water to the boil. Add the spaghetti and 1 tbsp of the olive oil and cook until tender, but still firm to the bite. Drain the spaghetti, return to the pan and sprinkle over the remaining olive oil. Cover, shake the pan, set aside and keep warm.

2 Pour the cream into a small saucepan and bring to simmering point, but do not let it boil. Pour the whisky or brandy into another small saucepan and bring to simmering point, but do not allow it to boil. Remove both pans from the heat and mix together the cream and whisky or brandy.

3 Cut the smoked salmon into thin strips and add to the cream mixture. Season to taste with cayenne and black pepper. Just before serving, stir in the chopped fresh coriander (cilantro) or parsley.

4 Transfer the spaghetti to a warm serving dish, pour over the sauce and toss thoroughly with 2 large forks. Scatter over the crumbled feta cheese, garnish with the coriander (cilantro) or parsley leaves and serve immediately.

COOK'S TIP

*Serve this rich and luxurious dish
with a green salad tossed in a
lemony dressing.*

Trout with Pasta Colle Acciughe & Smoked Bacon

*Most trout available nowadays is farmed rainbow trout,
however, if you can, buy wild brown trout for this recipe.*

Serves 4

INGREDIENTS

butter, for greasing
4 x 275 g/9¹/₂ oz trout, gutted
  and cleaned
12 anchovies in oil, drained
  and chopped
2 apples, peeled, cored and sliced

4 fresh mint sprigs
juice of 1 lemon
12 slices rindless smoked fatty bacon
450 g/1 lb dried tagliatelle
1 tbsp olive oil
salt and pepper

TO GARNISH:
2 apples, cored and sliced
4 fresh mint sprigs

1 Grease a deep baking (cookie) sheet with butter.

2 Open up the cavities of each trout and wash thoroughly with warm salt water.

3 Season each cavity with salt and black pepper. Divide the anchovies, sliced apples and mint sprigs between each of the cavities. Sprinkle the lemon juice into each cavity.

4 Carefully cover the whole of each trout, except the head and tail, with three slices of smoked bacon in a spiral.

5 Arrange the trout on the baking (cookie) sheet with the loose ends of bacon tucked underneath. Season with black pepper and bake in a preheated oven at 200°C/400°F/Gas 6 for 20 minutes, turning the trout over after 10 minutes.

6 Meanwhile, bring a large pan of lightly salted water to the boil. Add the tagliatelle and olive oil and cook for about 12 minutes, until tender but still firm to the bite. Drain the pasta and transfer to a large, warm serving dish.

7 Remove the trout from the oven and arrange on the tagliatelle. Garnish with sliced apples and fresh mint sprigs and serve immediately.

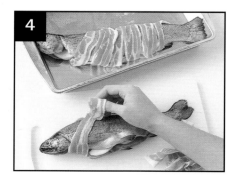

Farfalle with a Medley of Seafood

You can use almost any kind of sea fish in this recipe.
Red sea bream is an especially good choice.

Serves 4

INGREDIENTS

450 g/1 lb fillet of sea bream
60 g/2 oz/4 tbsp butter
12 scallops, shelled
12 raw tiger prawns (shrimp)
12 raw shrimp
125 g/4^1/$_2$ oz freshwater prawns
(shrimp)

juice and finely grated rind of
1 lemon
pinch of saffron powder or threads
1 litre/1^3/$_4$ pints/4 cups vegetable
stock
150 ml/^{1}/$_4$ pint/^{5}/$_8$ cup rose petal
vinegar (see page 98)
450 g/1 lb dried farfalle

1 tbsp olive oil
150 ml/^{1}/$_4$ pint/^{5}/$_8$ cup white wine
1 tbsp pink peppercorns
115 g/4 oz baby carrots
150 ml/^{1}/$_4$ pint/^{5}/$_8$ cup double
(heavy) cream or fromage frais
salt and pepper

1 Peel and devein the prawns (shrimp) and shrimp. Thinly slice the sea bream. Melt the butter in a pan, add the sea bream, scallops, prawns (shrimp) and shrimp and cook for 1–2 minutes.

2 Season with black pepper. Add the lemon juice and grated rind. Very carefully add a pinch of saffron powder or a few strands of saffron to the cooking juices (not to the seafood).

3 Remove the seafood from the pan, set aside and keep warm.

4 Return the pan to the heat and add the vegetable stock. Bring to the boil and reduce by one third. Add the rose petal vinegar and cook for 4 minutes, until reduced.

5 Bring a pan of salted water to the boil. Add the farfalle and olive oil and cook until tender, but still firm to the bite. Drain the pasta, transfer to a serving plate and top with the seafood.

6 Add the wine, peppercorns, and carrots to the pan and reduce the sauce for 6 minutes. Add the cream or fromage frais and simmer for 2 minutes.

7 Pour the sauce over the seafood and pasta and serve immediately.

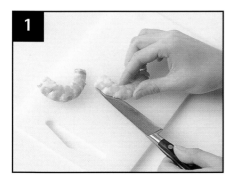

Seafood Lasagne

*This is one of those recipes where you can use any fish and any sauce you like:
from smoked finnan haddock with a little whisky sauce to cod with cheese sauce.*

Serves 4

INGREDIENTS

450 g/1 lb finnan haddock, filleted,
  skin removed and flesh flaked
115 g/ 4 oz prawns (shrimp)
115 g/4 oz sole fillet, skin removed
  and flesh sliced
juice of 1 lemon

60 g/2 oz/4 tbsp butter
3 leeks, very thinly sliced
60 g/2 oz/^{1}/$_2$ cup plain
  (all purpose) flour
about 600 ml/1 pint/2^1/$_3$ cups milk
2 tbsp clear honey

200g/7 oz /1^3/$_4$ cups grated
  mozzarella cheese
450g/1 lb pre-cooked lasagne
60 g/2 oz/^{2}/$_3$ cup freshly grated
  Parmesan cheese
black pepper

1 Put the haddock fillet, prawns (shrimp) and sole fillet into a large bowl and season with black pepper and lemon juice. Set aside while you start to make the sauce.

2 Melt the butter in a large saucepan. Add the leeks and cook, stirring occasionally, for 8 minutes. Add the flour and cook, stirring constantly, for 1 minute. Gradually stir in enough milk to make a thick, creamy sauce.

3 Blend in the honey and mozzarella cheese and cook for a further 3 minutes. Remove the pan from the heat and mix in the fish and prawns (shrimp).

4 Make alternate layers of fish sauce and lasagne in an ovenproof dish, finishing with a layer of fish sauce on top. Generously sprinkle over the grated Parmesan cheese and bake in a preheated oven at 180°C/ 350°F/Gas 4 for 30 minutes. Serve immediately.

VARIATION

*For a cider sauce, substitute
1 finely chopped shallot for the
leeks, 300 ml/½ pint/1¼ cups cider
and 300 ml/½ pint/1¼ cups double
(heavy) cream for the milk and
1 tsp mustard for the honey.
For a Tuscan sauce, substitute
1 finely chopped fennel bulb for the
leeks and omit the honey.*

Macaroni & Prawn (Shrimp) Bake

This adaptation of an eighteenth-century Italian dish is baked until
it is golden brown and sizzling, then cut into wedges like a cake.

Serves 4

INGREDIENTS

350 g/12 oz/3 cups dried short-
  cut macaroni
1 tbsp olive oil, plus extra
  for brushing
90 g/3 oz/6 tbsp butter, plus extra
  for greasing

2 small fennel bulbs, thinly sliced and
  fronds reserved
175 g/6 oz mushrooms, thinly sliced
175 g/6 oz peeled, cooked
  prawns (shrimp)
pinch of cayenne pepper

300 ml/^{1}/$_2$ pint/1^1/$_4$ cups Béchamel
  Sauce (see Cook's Tip, below)
60 g/2 oz/^{2}/$_3$ cup freshly grated
  Parmesan cheese
2 large tomatoes, sliced
1 tsp dried oregano
salt and pepper

1 Bring a saucepan of salted water to the boil. Add the pasta and oil and cook until tender, but still firm to the bite. Drain and return to the pan. Add 25 g/1 oz/2 tbsp of butter, cover, shake the pan and keep warm.

2 Melt the remaining butter in a saucepan. Fry the fennel for 3–4 minutes. Stir in the mushrooms and fry for a further 2 minutes. Stir in the prawns (shrimp), then remove the pan from the heat.

3 Stir the cayenne pepper and prawn (shrimp) mixture into the Béchamel sauce. Pour into a greased ovenproof dish and spread evenly. Sprinkle over the Parmesan cheese and arrange the tomato slices in a ring around the edge. Brush the tomatoes with olive oil and sprinkle over the oregano.

4 Bake in a preheated oven at 180°C/350°F/Gas 4 for 25 minutes, until golden brown. Serve immediately.

COOK'S TIP

For Béchamel sauce, melt 25 g/
1 oz/2 tbsp butter. Stir in 25 g/
1 oz/¼ cup flour. Cook, stirring, for
2 minutes. Gradually, stir in
300 ml/½ pint/1¼ cups warm
milk. Add 2 tbsp finely chopped
onion, 5 white peppercorns and
2 parsley sprigs and season with
salt, dried thyme and grated
nutmeg. Simmer, stirring, for
15 minutes. Strain before using.

Farfallini Buttered Lobster

This is one of those dishes that looks almost too lovely to eat – but you should!

Serves 4

INGREDIENTS

2 x 700 g/1 lb 9 oz lobsters, split
　into halves
juice and grated rind of 1 lemon
115 g/4 oz/¹/₂ cup butter
4 tbsp fresh white breadcrumbs
2 tbsp brandy

5 tbsp double (heavy) cream
　or crème fraîche
450 g/ 1 lb dried farfallini
1 tbsp olive oil
60 g/2 oz/²/₃ cup freshly grated
　Parmesan cheese
salt and pepper

TO GARNISH:
1 kiwi fruit, sliced
4 unpeeled, cooked king prawns
　(shrimp)
fresh dill sprigs

1 Carefully discard the stomach sac, vein and gills from each lobster. Remove all the meat from the tail and chop. Crack the claws and legs, remove the meat and chop. Transfer the meat to a bowl and add the lemon juice and grated lemon rind.

2 Clean the shells thoroughly and place in a warm oven at 170°C/325°/Gas 3 to dry out.

3 Melt 25 g/1 oz/2 tbsp of the butter in a frying pan (skillet). Add the breadcrumbs and fry for about 3 minutes, until crisp and golden brown.

4 Melt the remaining butter in a saucepan. Add the lobster meat and heat through gently. Add the brandy and cook for a further 3 minutes, then add the cream or crème fraîche and season to taste with salt and black pepper.

5 Meanwhile, bring a large pan of lightly salted water to the boil. Add the farfallini and olive oil and cook for about 12 minutes, until tender but still firm to the bite. Drain and spoon the pasta into the clean lobster shells. Top with the buttered lobster and sprinkle with a little grated Parmesan cheese and the breadcrumbs. Grill (broil) for 2–3 minutes, until golden brown.

6 Transfer the lobster shells to a warm serving dish, garnish with the lemon slices, kiwi fruit, king prawns (shrimp) and dill sprigs and serve immediately.

Pasta Shells with Mussels

Serve this aromatic seafood dish to family and friends who admit to a love of garlic.

Serves 4–6

INGREDIENTS

1.25 kg/2³/₄ lb mussels
225 ml/8 fl oz/1 cup dry white wine
2 large onions, chopped
115 g/4 oz/¹/₂ cup unsalted butter

6 large garlic cloves, finely chopped
5 tbsp chopped fresh parsley
300 ml/¹/₂ pint/1¹/₄ cups double (heavy) cream

400 g/14 oz dried pasta shells
1 tbsp olive oil
salt and pepper
crusty bread, to serve

1 Scrub and debeard the mussels under cold running water. Discard any that do not close immediately when sharply tapped. Put the mussels into a large saucepan, together with the wine and half of the onions. Cover and cook over a medium heat, shaking the pan frequently, for 2–3 minutes, until the shells open.

2 Remove the pan from the heat. Drain the mussels and reserve the cooking liquid. Discard any mussels that have not opened. Strain the cooking liquid through a clean cloth into a glass jug (pitcher) or bowl and reserve.

3 Melt the butter in a pan over a medium heat. Add the remaining onion and fry until translucent. Stir in the garlic and cook for 1 minute. Gradually stir in the reserved cooking liquid. Stir in the parsley and cream and season to taste with salt and black pepper. Bring to simmering point over a low heat.

4 Meanwhile, bring a large saucepan of lightly salted water to the boil. Add the pasta and olive oil and cook until just tender, but still firm to the bite. Drain the pasta, return to the pan, cover and keep warm.

5 Reserve a few mussels for the garnish and remove the remainder from their shells. Stir the shelled mussels into the cream sauce and warm briefly.

6 Transfer the pasta to a large, warm serving dish. Pour over the sauce and toss well to coat. Garnish with the reserved mussels and serve with warm, crusty bread.

COOK'S TIP

Pasta shells are ideal because the sauce collects in the cavities and impregnates the pasta with flavour.

Saffron Mussel Tagliatelle

*Saffron is the most expensive spice in the world, but you only ever need
a small quantity. Saffron threads or powdered saffron may be used in this recipe.*

Serves 4

INGREDIENTS

1 kg/2¼ lb mussels
150 ml/¼ pint/⅝ cup white wine
1 medium onion, finely chopped
25 g/1 oz/2 tbsp butter
2 garlic cloves, crushed
2 tsp cornflour (cornstarch)

300 ml/½ pint/1¼ cups double
　(heavy) cream
pinch of saffron threads or
　saffron powder
juice of ½ lemon
1 egg yolk

450 g/1 lb dried tagliatelle
1 tbsp olive oil
salt and pepper
3 tbsp chopped fresh parsley,
　to garnish

1 Scrub and debeard the mussels under cold running water. Discard any that do not close when sharply tapped. Put the mussels in a pan with the wine and onion. Cover and cook over a high heat, shaking the pan, for 5–8 minutes, until the shells open.

2 Drain and reserve the cooking liquid. Discard any mussels that are still closed. Reserve a few mussels for the garnish and remove the remainder from their shells.

3 Strain the cooking liquid into a saucepan. Bring to the boil and reduce by about half. Remove the pan from the heat.

4 Melt the butter in a saucepan. Add the garlic and cook, stirring frequently, for 2 minutes, until golden brown. Stir in the cornflour (cornstarch) and cook, stirring, for 1 minute. Gradually stir in the cooking liquid and the cream. Crush the saffron threads and add to the pan. Season with salt and pepper to taste and

simmer over a low heat for 2–3 minutes, until thickened.

5 Stir in the egg yolk, lemon juice and shelled mussels. Do not allow the mixture to boil.

6 Meanwhile, bring a pan of salted water to the boil. Add the pasta and oil and cook until tender, but still firm to the bite. Drain and transfer to a serving dish. Add the mussel sauce and toss. Garnish with the parsley and reserved mussels and serve.

Baked Scallops with Pasta in Shells

This is another tempting seafood dish where the eye is delighted as much as the tastebuds.

Serves 4

INGREDIENTS

12 scallops
3 tbsp olive oil
350 g/12 oz/3 cups small, dried
   wholemeal (whole-wheat)
   pasta shells

150 ml/¼ pint/⅝ cup fish stock
1 onion, chopped
juice and finely grated rind of
   2 lemons
150 ml/¼ pint/⅝ cup double
   (heavy) cream

225 g/8 oz/2 cups grated
   Cheddar cheese
salt and pepper
crusty brown bread, to serve

1 Remove the scallops from their shells. Scrape off the skirt and the black intestinal thread. Reserve the white part (the flesh) and the orange part (the coral or roe). Very carefully ease the flesh and coral from the shell with a short, but very strong knife.

2 Wash the shells thoroughly and dry them well. Put the shells on a baking (cookie) sheet, sprinkle lightly with about two thirds of the olive oil and set aside.

3 Meanwhile, bring a large saucepan of lightly salted water to the boil. Add the pasta shells and remaining olive oil and cook for about 12 minutes, until tender, but still firm to the bite. Drain and spoon about 25 g/1 oz of pasta into each scallop shell.

4 Put the scallops, fish stock and onion in an ovenproof dish and season to taste with pepper. Cover with foil and bake in a preheated oven at 180°C/ 350°F/Gas 4 for 8 minutes.

5 Remove the dish from the oven. Remove the foil and, using a slotted spoon, transfer the scallops to the shells. Add 1 tbsp of the cooking liquid to each shell, together with a drizzle of lemon juice and a little cream, and top with the grated cheese.

6 Increase the oven temperature to 230°C/450°F/Gas 8 and return the scallops to the oven for a further 4 minutes.

7 Serve the scallops in their shells with crusty brown bread and butter.

Vermicelli with Clams

A quickly cooked recipe that transforms store-cupboard ingredients into a dish with style.

Serves 4

INGREDIENTS

400 g/14 oz dried vermicelli,
   spaghetti or other long pasta
2 tbsp olive oil
25 g/1 oz/2 tbsp butter
2 onions, chopped

2 garlic cloves, chopped
2 x 200 g/7 oz jars clams in brine
125 ml/4 fl oz/$\frac{1}{2}$ cup white wine
4 tbsp chopped fresh parsley
$\frac{1}{2}$ tsp dried oregano

pinch of freshly grated nutmeg
salt and pepper

TO GARNISH:
2 tbsp Parmesan cheese shavings
fresh basil sprigs

1 Bring a large pan of lightly salted water to the boil. Add the pasta and half the olive oil and cook until tender, but still firm to the bite. Drain, return to the pan and add the butter. Cover the pan, shake well and keep warm.

2 Heat the remaining oil in a pan over a medium heat. Add the onions and fry until they are translucent. Stir in the garlic and cook for 1 minute.

3 Strain the liquid from 1 jar of clams and add the liquid to the pan, with the wine. Stir, bring to simmering point and simmer for 3 minutes. Drain the second jar of clams and discard the liquid.

4 Add the clams, parsley and oregano to the pan and season with pepper and nutmeg. Lower the heat and cook until the sauce is heated through.

5 Transfer the pasta to a warm serving dish and pour over the sauce. Sprinkle with the Parmesan cheese, garnish with the basil and serve immediately.

COOK'S TIP

There are many different types of clams found along almost every coast in the world. Those traditionally used in this dish are the tiny ones – only 2.5–5 cm/ 1–2 inches across – known in Italy as vongole.

Squid & Macaroni Stew

This scrumptious seafood dish is quick and easy to make, yet deliciously satisfying to eat.

Serves 4–6

INGREDIENTS

225 g/8 oz/2 cups dried short-cut macaroni or other small pasta shapes
7 tbsp olive oil
2 onions, sliced

350 g/12 oz prepared squid, cut into 4 cm/1^1/$_2$ inch strips
225 ml/8 fl oz/1 cup fish stock
150 ml/^{1}/$_4$ pint/^{5}/$_8$ cup red wine
350 g/12 oz tomatoes, skinned and thinly sliced

2 tbsp tomato purée (paste)
1 tsp dried oregano
2 bay leaves
2 tbsp chopped fresh parsley
salt and pepper
crusty bread, to serve

1 Bring a large saucepan of lightly salted water to the boil. Add the pasta and 1 tbsp of the olive oil and cook for 3 minutes. Drain, return to the pan, cover and keep warm.

2 Heat the remaining oil in a pan over a medium heat. Add the onions and fry until they are translucent. Add the squid and stock and simmer for 5 minutes. Pour in the wine and add the tomatoes, tomato purée (paste), oregano and bay leaves. Bring the

sauce to the boil, season to taste and cook for 5 minutes.

3 Stir the pasta into the pan, cover and simmer for about 10 minutes, or until the squid and macaroni are tender and the sauce has thickened. If the sauce remains too liquid, uncover the pan and continue cooking for a few minutes.

4 Remove and discard the bay leaves. Reserve a little parsley and stir the remainder into the pan. Transfer to a warm serving

dish and sprinkle over the remaining parsley. Serve with crusty bread to soak up the sauce.

COOK'S TIP

To prepare squid, peel off the outer skin, then cut off the head and tentacles. Extract the transparent flat oval bone from the body and discard. Remove the sac of black ink, then turn the body sac inside out. Wash in cold water. Cut off the tentacles and discard the rest; wash thoroughly.

Vegetables & Salads

The pasta recipes in this chapter offer something special for every occasion: filling vegetarian suppers, unusual vegetable side dishes, main course and side salads. You could even take many of the salads on a picnic and, of course, they are perfect as accompaniments for summer barbecues. Some are classic dishes, such as Fettuccine all'Alfredo, Spaghetti Olio e Aglio, Paglia e Fieno and Pasta & Herring Salad. Others are imaginative and sometimes surprising new combinations of vegetables and pasta. Try Mediterranean Spaghetti, Spinach & Wild Mushroom Lasagne, Ravioli with Vegetable Stuffing and Rare Beef Pasta Salad for a family meal, while Linguine with Braised Fennel, Goat's Cheese with Penne & Walnut Salad and Pasta & Garlic Mayo Salad make superb side dishes to get the tastebuds tingling.

Fettuccine all'Alfredo

This simple, traditional dish can be made with any long pasta,
but is especially good with flat noodles, such as fettuccine or tagliatelle.

Serves 4

INGREDIENTS

25 g/1 oz/2 tbsp butter
200 ml/7 fl oz/$^7/_8$ cup double
   (heavy) cream
460 g/1 lb fresh fettuccine

1 tbsp olive oil
90 g/3 oz/1 cup freshly grated
   Parmesan cheese, plus extra
   to serve

pinch of freshly grated nutmeg
salt and pepper
fresh parsley sprigs, to garnish

1 Put the butter and 150 ml/ ¼ pint/$^5/_8$ cup of the cream in a large saucepan and bring the mixture to the boil over a medium heat. Reduce the heat and then simmer gently for about 1½ minutes, or until slightly thickened.

2 Meanwhile, bring a large pan of lightly salted water to the boil. Add the fettuccine and olive oil and cook for 2–3 minutes, until tender but still firm to the bite. Drain the fettuccine thoroughly and then pour over the cream sauce.

3 Toss the fettuccine in the sauce over a low heat until thoroughly coated.

4 Add the remaining cream, the Parmesan cheese and nutmeg to the fettuccine mixture and season to taste with salt and pepper. Toss thoroughly to coat while gently heating through.

5 Transfer the fettuccine mixture to a warm serving plate and garnish with the fresh sprig of parsley. Serve immediately, handing extra grated Parmesan cheese separately.

VARIATION

This classic Roman dish is often served with the addition of strips of ham and fresh peas. Add 225 g/ 8 oz/2 cups shelled cooked peas and 175 g/6 oz ham strips with the Parmesan cheese in step 4.

Macaroni Bake

*This satisfying dish would make an
excellent supper for a mid-week family meal.*

Serves 4

INGREDIENTS

460 g/1 lb/4 cups dried short-
  cut macaroni
1 tbsp olive oil
60 g/2 oz/4 tbsp beef dripping

460 g/1 lb potatoes, thinly sliced
460 g/1 lb onions, sliced
225 g/8 oz/2 cups grated
  mozzarella cheese

150 ml/5 fl oz/⁵⁄₈ cup double
  (heavy) cream
salt and pepper
crusty brown bread and butter, to serve

1 Bring a large saucepan of
lightly salted water to the
boil. Add the macaroni and olive
oil and cook for about 12 minutes,
until tender but still firm to the
bite. Drain the macaroni
thoroughly and set aside.

2 Melt the dripping in a large
flameproof casserole, then
remove from the heat.

3 Make alternate layers of
potatoes, onions, macaroni
and grated cheese in the dish,
seasoning well with salt and
pepper between each layer and

finishing with a layer of cheese on
top. Finally, pour the cream over
the top layer of cheese.

4 Bake in a preheated oven at
200°C/400°F/Gas 6 for
25 minutes. Remove the dish from
the oven and carefully brown the
top of the bake under a hot grill
(broiler).

5 Serve the bake straight from
the dish with crusty brown
bread and butter as a main course.
Alternatively, serve as a vegetable
accompaniment with your
favourite main course.

VARIATION

For a stronger flavour, use
mozzarella affumicata, *a smoked
version of this cheese, or* Gruyère
*(Swiss) cheese instead of
the mozzarella.*

Creamy Pasta & Broccoli

This colourful dish provides a mouth-watering contrast in the crisp 'al dente' texture of the broccoli and the creamy cheese sauce.

Serves 4

INGREDIENTS

60 g/2 oz/4 tbsp butter
1 large onion, finely chopped
450 g/1 lb dried ribbon pasta
460 g/1 lb broccoli, broken into
  florets (flowerets)

150 ml/$\frac{1}{4}$ pint/$\frac{5}{8}$ cup boiling
  vegetable stock
1 tbsp plain (all purpose) flour
150 ml/$\frac{1}{4}$ pint/$\frac{5}{8}$ cup single
  (light) cream

60 g/2 oz/$\frac{1}{2}$ cup grated
  mozzarella cheese
freshly grated nutmeg
salt and white pepper
fresh apple slices, to garnish

1 Melt half of the butter in a large saucepan over a medium heat. Add the onion and fry for 4 minutes.

2 Add the broccoli and pasta to the pan and cook, stirring constantly, for 2 minutes. Add the vegetable stock, bring back to the boil and simmer for a further 12 minutes. Season well with salt and white pepper.

3 Meanwhile, melt the remaining butter in a saucepan over a medium heat.

Sprinkle over the flour and cook, stirring constantly, for 2 minutes. Gradually stir in the cream and bring to simmering point, but do not boil. Add the grated cheese and season with salt and a little freshly grated nutmeg.

4 Drain the pasta and broccoli mixture and pour over the cheese sauce. Cook, stirring occasionally, for about 2 minutes. Transfer the pasta and broccoli mixture to a warm, large, deep serving dish and serve garnished with slices of fresh apple.

VARIATION

This dish would also be delicious and look just as colourful made with Cape broccoli, which is actually a purple variety of cauliflower and not broccoli at all.

Paglia e Fieno

The name of this dish – 'straw and hay' –
refers to the colours of the pasta when mixed together.

Serves 4

INGREDIENTS

60 g/2 oz/4 tbsp butter
900 g/1 lb fresh peas, shelled
200 ml/7 fl oz/⁷⁄₈ cup double
    (heavy) cream

460 g/1 lb mixed fresh green and
    white spaghetti or tagliatelle
1 tbsp olive oil

60 g/2 oz/²⁄₃ cup freshly grated
    Parmesan cheese, plus extra to serve
pinch of freshly grated nutmeg
salt and pepper

1 Melt the butter in a large saucepan. Add the peas and cook, over a low heat, for 2–3 minutes.

2 Using a measuring jug (pitcher), pour 150 ml/ 5 fl oz/⁵⁄₈ cup of the cream into the pan, bring to the boil and simmer for 1–1½ minutes, until slightly thickened. Remove the pan from the heat.

3 Meanwhile, bring a large pan of lightly salted water to the boil. Add the spaghetti or tagliatelle and olive oil and cook for 2–3 minutes, until just tender but still firm to the bite. Remove the pan from the heat, drain the pasta thoroughly and return to the pan.

4 Add the peas and cream sauce to the pasta. Return the pan to the heat and add the remaining cream and the Parmesan cheese and season to taste with salt, black pepper and grated nutmeg.

5 Using 2 forks, gently toss the pasta to coat with the peas and cream sauce, while heating through.

6 Transfer the pasta to a serving dish and serve immediately, with extra Parmesan cheese.

VARIATION

Fry 140 g/5 oz/2 cups sliced button or oyster mushrooms in 60 g/2 oz/4 tbsp butter over a low heat for 4–5 minutes. Stir into the peas and cream sauce just before adding to the pasta in step 4.

Green Tagliatelle with Garlic

A rich pasta dish for garlic lovers everywhere.
It is quick and easy to prepare and full of flavour.

Serves 4

INGREDIENTS

2 tbsp walnut oil
1 bunch spring onions
   (scallions), sliced
2 garlic cloves, thinly sliced
250 g/8 oz/3^1/4 cups sliced
   mushrooms
450 g/1 lb fresh green and white
   tagliatelle

1 tbsp olive oil
225 g/8 oz frozen spinach, thawed
   and drained
115 g/4 oz/^{1}/2 cup full-fat soft
   cheese with garlic and herbs
4 tbsp single (light) cream
60 g/2 oz/^{1}/2 cup chopped, unsalted
   pistachio nuts

salt and pepper

TO GARNISH:
2 tbsp shredded fresh basil
fresh basil sprigs
Italian bread, to serve

1 Heat the walnut oil in a large frying pan (skillet). Add the spring onions (scallions) and garlic and fry for 1 minute, until just softened.

2 Add the mushrooms to the pan, stir well, cover and cook over a low heat for about 5 minutes, until softened.

3 Meanwhile, bring a large saucepan of lightly salted water to the boil. Add the

tagliatelle and olive oil and cook for 3–5 minutes, until tender but still firm to the bite. Drain the tagliatelle thoroughly and return to the saucepan.

4 Add the spinach to the frying pan (skillet) and heat through for 1–2 minutes. Add the cheese to the pan and allow to melt slightly. Stir in the cream and continue to cook, without allowing the mixture to come to the boil, until warmed through.

5 Pour the sauce over the pasta, season to taste with salt and black pepper and mix well. Heat through gently, stirring constantly, for 2–3 minutes.

6 Transfer the pasta to a serving dish and sprinkle with the pistachio nuts and shredded basil. Garnish with the basil sprigs and serve immediately with the Italian bread of your choice.

Spaghetti Olio e Aglio

*This easy and satisfying Roman dish originated as a cheap meal for poor people,
but has now become a favourite in restaurants and trattorias.*

Serves 4

INGREDIENTS

125 ml/4 fl oz/$^{1}/_{2}$ cup olive oil
3 garlic cloves, crushed

460 g/1 lb fresh spaghetti

3 tbsp roughly chopped fresh parsley
salt and pepper

1 Reserve 1 tbsp of the olive oil and heat the remainder in a medium saucepan. Add the garlic and a pinch of salt and cook over a low heat, stirring constantly, until golden brown, then remove the pan from the heat. Do not allow the garlic to burn as it will taint its flavour. (If it does burn, you will have to start all over again!)

2 Meanwhile, bring a large saucepan of lightly salted water to the boil. Add the spaghetti and remaining olive oil and cook for 2–3 minutes, until tender, but still firm to the bite. Drain the spaghetti thoroughly and return to the pan.

3 Add the oil and garlic mixture to the spaghetti and toss to coat thoroughly. Season with pepper, add the chopped fresh parsley and toss to coat again.

4 Transfer the spaghetti to a warm serving dish and serve immediately.

COOK'S TIP

Oils produced by different countries, mainly Italy, Spain and Greece, have their own characteristic flavours. Some produce an oil which has a hot, peppery taste while others have a 'green' flavour.

COOK'S TIP

It is worth buying the best-quality olive oil for dishes such as this one which makes a feature of its flavour, and for salad dressings in addition. Extra virgin oil is produced from the first pressing and has the lowest acidity. It is more expensive than other types of olive oil, but has the finest flavour. Virgin olive oil is slightly more acid, but is also well flavoured. Oil simply labelled pure has usually been heat-treated and refined by mechanical means and, consequently, lacks character and flavour.

Patriotic Pasta

*The ingredients of this dish have the same
bright colours as the Italian flag – hence its name.*

Serves 4

INGREDIENTS

460 g/1 lb/4 cups dried farfalle
4 tbsp olive oil

460 g/1 lb cherry tomatoes
90 g/3 oz rocket (arugula)

salt and pepper
Pecorino cheese, to garnish

1 Bring a large saucepan of lightly salted water to the boil. Add the farfalle and 1 tbsp of the olive oil and cook until tender, but still firm to the bite. Drain the farfalle thoroughly and return to the pan.

2 Cut the cherry tomatoes in half and trim the rocket (arugula).

3 Heat the remaining olive oil in a large saucepan. Add the tomatoes and cook for 1 minute. Add the farfalle and the rocket (arugula) and stir gently to mix. Heat through and season to taste with salt and black pepper.

4 Meanwhile, using a vegetable peeler, shave thin slices of Pecorino cheese.

5 Transfer the farfalle and vegetables to a warm serving dish. Garnish with the Pecorino cheese shavings and serve immediately.

COOK'S TIP

Pecorino cheese is a hard sheep's milk cheese which resembles Parmesan and is often used for grating over a variety of dishes. It has a sharp flavour and is only used in small quantities.

COOK'S TIP

Rocket (arugula) is a small plant with irregular-shaped leaves rather like those of turnip tops (greens). The flavour is distinctively peppery and slightly reminiscent of radish. It has always been popular in Italy, both in salads and for serving with pasta and has recently enjoyed a revival in Britain and the United States, where it has now become very fashionable.

Mediterranean Spaghetti

*Delicious Mediterranean vegetables, cooked in rich tomato sauce,
make an ideal topping for nutty wholemeal (whole-wheat) pasta.*

Serves 4

INGREDIENTS

2 tbsp olive oil
1 large, red onion, chopped
2 garlic cloves, crushed
1 tbsp lemon juice
4 baby aubergines (eggplant),
   quartered

600 ml/1 pint/2^1/$_2$ cups passata
   (sieved tomatoes)
2 tsp caster (superfine) sugar
2 tbsp tomato purée (paste)
400 g/14 oz can artichoke hearts,
   drained and halved

115 g/4 oz/1 cup stoned (pitted)
   black olives
350 g/12 oz dried spaghetti
25 g/1 oz/2 tbsp butter
salt and pepper
fresh basil sprigs, to garnish
olive bread, to serve

1 Heat 1 tbsp of the olive oil in a large frying pan (skillet). Add the onion, garlic, lemon juice and aubergines (eggplant) and cook over a low heat for 4–5 minutes, until the onion and aubergines (eggplant) are lightly golden brown.

2 Pour in the passata (sieved tomatoes), season to taste with salt and black pepper and stir in the caster (superfine) sugar and tomato purée (paste). Bring to the boil, lower the heat and then simmer, stirring occasionally, for 20 minutes.

3 Gently stir in the artichoke hearts and black olives and cook for 5 minutes.

4 Meanwhile, bring a large saucepan of lightly salted water to the boil. Add the spaghetti and the remaining oil and cook for 7–8 minutes, until tender but still firm to the bite.

5 Drain the spaghetti thoroughly and toss with the butter. Transfer the spaghetti to a large serving dish.

6 Pour the vegetable sauce over the spaghetti, garnish with the sprigs of fresh basil and serve immediately with olive bread.

Spinach & Wild Mushroom Lasagne

This is one of the tastiest vegetarian dishes. Always check the seasoning of vegetables, as it is most important. You can always add a little more seasoning to a recipe, but you cannot take it out once it has been added.

Serves 4

INGREDIENTS

115 g/4 oz/8 tbsp butter, plus extra
  for greasing
2 garlic cloves, finely chopped
115 g/4 oz shallots
225 g/8 oz wild mushrooms, such as
  chanterelles

450 g/1 lb spinach, cooked, drained
  and finely chopped
225 g/8 oz/2 cups grated
  Cheddar cheese
1/4 tsp freshly grated nutmeg
1 tsp chopped fresh basil

60 g/2 oz plain (all purpose) flour
600 ml/1 pint/2 1/2 cups hot milk
60 g/2 oz/ 2/3 cup grated Cheshire
  cheese
salt and pepper
8 sheets pre-cooked lasagne

1 Lightly grease an ovenproof dish with a little butter.

2 Melt 60 g/2 oz/4 tbsp of the butter in a saucepan. Add the garlic, shallots and wild mushrooms and fry over a low heat for 3 minutes. Stir in the spinach, Cheddar cheese, nutmeg and basil. Season well with salt and black pepper and set aside.

3 Melt the remaining butter in another saucepan over a low heat. Add the flour and cook, stirring constantly, for 1 minute. Gradually stir in the hot milk, whisking constantly until smooth. Stir in 25 g/1 oz/1/4 cup of the Cheshire cheese and season to taste with salt and black pepper.

4 Spread half of the mushroom and spinach mixture over the base of the prepared dish. Cover with a layer of lasagne and then with half of the cheese sauce. Repeat the process and sprinkle over the remaining Cheshire cheese. Bake in a preheated oven at 200°C/400°F/Gas 6 for 30 minutes, until golden brown.

VARIATION

You could substitute 4 (bell) peppers for the spinach. Roast in a preheated oven at 200°C/400°F/ Gas Mark 6 for 20 minutes. Rub off the skins under cold water, deseed and chop before using.

Ravioli with Vegetable Stuffing

It is important not to overcook the vegetable filling or it will become sloppy and unexciting, instead of firm to the bite and delicious.

Serves 4

INGREDIENTS

450 g/1 lb Basic Pasta Dough (see page 4)
1 tbsp olive oil
90 g/3 oz/6 tbsp butter
150 ml/5 fl oz/⅝ cup single (light) cream
75 g/3 oz/1 cup freshly grated Parmesan cheese

STUFFING:
2 large aubergines (eggplant)
3 large courgettes (zucchini)
6 large tomatoes
1 large green (bell) pepper
1 large red (bell) pepper
3 garlic cloves
1 large onion

120 ml/4 fl oz/½ cup olive oil
60 g/2 oz tomato purée (paste)
½ tsp chopped fresh basil
salt and pepper

1 To make the stuffing, cut the aubergines (eggplant) and courgettes (zucchini) into 2.5 cm/1 inch chunks. Put the aubergine (eggplant) pieces in a colander, sprinkle with salt and set aside for 20 minutes. Rinse and drain.

2 Blanch the tomatoes in boiling water for 2 minutes. Drain, skin and chop the flesh. Core and seed the (bell) peppers and cut into 2.5 cm/1 inch dice. Chop the garlic and onion.

3 Heat the oil in a saucepan. Add the garlic and onion and fry for 3 minutes. Stir in the aubergines (eggplant), courgettes (zucchini), tomatoes, (bell) peppers, tomato purée (paste) and basil. Season with salt and pepper, cover and simmer for 20 minutes, stirring frequently.

4 Roll out the pasta dough and cut out 7.5 cm/3 inch rounds with a plain cutter. Put a spoonful of the vegetable stuffing on each

round. Dampen the edges slightly and fold the pasta rounds over, pressing together to seal.

5 Bring a saucepan of salted water to the boil. Add the ravioli and the oil and cook for 3–4 minutes. Drain and transfer to a greased ovenproof dish, dotting each layer with butter. Pour over the cream and sprinkle over the Parmesan cheese. Bake in a preheated oven at 200°C/400°F/Gas 6 for 20 minutes. Serve hot.

Courgette (Zucchini) & Aubergine (Eggplant) Lasagne

This rich, baked pasta dish is packed full of vegetables,
tomatoes and Italian mozzarella cheese.

Serves 6

INGREDIENTS

1 kg/2 ^{1}/$_4$ lb aubergines (eggplant)
8 tbsp olive oil
25 g/1/ oz/2 tbsp garlic and herb butter
450 g/1 lb courgettes (zucchini), sliced

225 g/8 oz/2 cups grated mozzarella cheese
600 ml/1 pint/2^1/$_2$ cups passata (sieved tomatoes)
6 sheets pre-cooked green lasagne

600 ml/1 pint/2^1/$_2$ cups Béchamel Sauce (see page 166)
60 g/2 oz/^{2}/$_3$ cup freshly grated Parmesan cheese
1 tsp dried oregano
salt and black pepper

1 Thinly slice the aubergines (eggplant) and place in a colander. Sprinkle with salt and set aside for 20 minutes. Rinse and pat dry with kitchen paper.

2 Heat 4 tbsp of the oil in a large frying pan (skillet). Fry half the aubergine (eggplant) slices over a low heat for 6–7 minutes, until golden. Drain on kitchen paper. Repeat with the remaining oil and aubergine (eggplant) slices.

3 Melt the garlic and herb butter in the frying pan (skillet). Add the courgettes (zucchini) and fry for 5–6 minutes, until golden brown all over. Drain on kitchen paper.

4 Place half the aubergine (eggplant) and courgette (zucchini) slices in a large ovenproof dish. Season with pepper and sprinkle over half the mozzarella cheese. Spoon over half

the passata (sieved tomatoes) and top with 3 sheets of lasagne. Repeat the process, ending with a layer of lasagne.

5 Spoon over the Béchamel sauce and sprinkle over the Parmesan cheese and oregano. Put the dish on a baking (cookie) sheet and bake in a preheated oven at 220°C/425°F/Gas 7 for 30–35 minutes, until golden brown. Serve immediately.

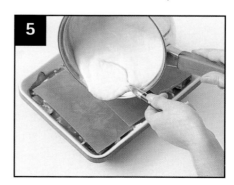

Pasta & Bean Casserole

A satisfying winter dish, pasta and bean casserole with a crunchy topping is a slow-cooked, one-pot meal.

Serves 6

INGREDIENTS

225 g/8 oz/1^1/$_4$ cups dried haricot (navy) beans, soaked overnight and drained
225 g/8 oz dried penne
6 tbsp olive oil
850 ml/1^1/$_2$ pints /3^1/$_2$ cups vegetable stock
2 large onions, sliced

2 garlic cloves, chopped
2 bay leaves
1 tsp dried oregano
1 tsp dried thyme
5 tbsp red wine
2 tbsp tomato purée (paste)
2 celery sticks (stalks), sliced
1 fennel bulb, sliced

115 g/4 oz/1^5/$_8$ cups sliced mushrooms
250 g/8 oz tomatoes, sliced
1 tsp dark muscovado sugar
4 tbsp dry white breadcrumbs
salt and pepper
salad leaves (greens) and crusty bread, to serve

1 Put the haricot (navy) beans in a large saucepan and add sufficient cold water to cover. Bring to the boil and continue to boil vigorously for 20 minutes. Drain, set aside and keep warm.

2 Bring a large saucepan of lightly salted water to the boil. Add the penne and 1 tbsp of the olive oil and cook for about 3 minutes. Drain the pasta, set aside and keep warm.

3 Put the beans in a large, flameproof casserole. Add the vegetable stock and stir in the remaining olive oil, the onions, garlic, bay leaves, oregano, thyme, wine and tomato purée (paste). Bring to the boil, then cover and cook in a preheated oven at 180°C/350°F/Gas 4 for 2 hours.

4 Add the penne, celery, fennel, mushrooms and tomatoes to the casserole and season to taste

with salt and pepper. Stir in the muscovado sugar and sprinkle over the breadcrumbs. Cover the dish and cook in the oven for 1 further hour.

5 Serve hot with salad leaves (greens) and crusty bread.

Creamed Spaghetti & Mushrooms

*This easy vegetarian dish is ideal for busy people
with little time, but good taste!*

Serves 4

INGREDIENTS

60 g/2 oz/4 tbsp butter
2 tbsp olive oil
6 shallots, sliced
450 g/1 lb/6 cups sliced
   button mushrooms
1 tsp plain (all purpose) flour

150 ml/¼ pint/⅝ cup double
   (heavy) cream
2 tbsp port
115 g/4 oz sun-dried
   tomatoes, chopped
freshly grated nutmeg

450g /1 lb dried spaghetti
1 tbsp freshly chopped parsley
salt and pepper
6 triangles of fried white bread,
   to serve

1 Heat the butter and 1 tbsp of the oil in a large saucepan. Add the shallots and cook over a medium heat for 3 minutes. Add the mushrooms and cook over a low heat for 2 minutes. Season with salt and black pepper, sprinkle over the flour and cook, stirring constantly, for 1 minute.

2 Gradually stir in the cream and port, add the sun-dried tomatoes and a pinch of grated nutmeg and cook over a low heat for 8 minutes.

3 Meanwhile bring a large saucepan of lightly salted water to the boil. Add the spaghetti and remaining olive oil and cook for 12–14 minutes, until tender but still firm to the bite.

4 Drain the spaghetti and return to the pan. Pour over the mushroom sauce and cook for 3 minutes. Transfer the spaghetti and mushroom sauce to a large serving plate and sprinkle over the chopped parsley. Serve with crispy triangles of fried bread.

VARIATION

Non-vegetarians could add 115 g/ 4 oz Parma ham (prosciutto), cut into thin strips and heated gently in 25 g/1 oz/2 tbsp butter, to the pasta along with the mushroom sauce.

Vegetable Pasta Stir-fry

*Prepare all the vegetables and cook the pasta in advance,
then the dish can be cooked in a few minutes.*

Serves 4

INGREDIENTS

400 g/14 oz dried wholemeal (whole-
  wheat) pasta shells or other short
  pasta shapes
1 tbsp olive oil
2 carrots, thinly sliced
115 g/4 oz baby corn cobs
3 tbsp corn oil
2.5 cm/1 inch piece fresh root ginger,
  thinly sliced

1 large onion, thinly sliced
1 garlic clove, thinly sliced
3 celery sticks (stalks), thinly sliced
1 small red (bell) pepper, cored,
  seeded and cut into matchstick
  strips
1 small green (bell) pepper, cored,
  seeded and cut into matchstick
  strips

1 tsp cornflour (cornstarch)
2 tbsp water
3 tbsp soy sauce
3 tbsp dry sherry
1 tsp clear honey
a dash of hot pepper sauce (optional)
salt

1 Bring a large saucepan of
lightly salted water to the
boil. Add the pasta and olive oil
and cook until tender, but still
firm to the bite. Drain, return to
the pan and keep warm.

2 Bring a saucepan of lightly
salted water to the boil. Add
the carrots and corn cobs and cook
for 2 minutes. Drain, refresh in
cold water and drain again.

3 Heat the corn oil in a
preheated wok or large frying
pan (skillet). Add the ginger and
stir-fry over a medium heat for
1 minute to flavour the oil.
Remove the ginger with a slotted
spoon and discard.

4 Add the onion, garlic, celery
and (bell) peppers to the pan
and stir-fry for 2 minutes. Add the
carrots and baby corn cobs and

stir-fry for a further 2 minutes. Stir
in the drained pasta.

5 Mix together the cornflour
(cornstarch) and water to
make a smooth paste. Stir in the
soy sauce, sherry and honey. Pour
the cornflour mixture into the pasta
and cook, stirring occasionally, for
2 minutes. Stir in a dash of pepper
sauce, if liked. Transfer to a serving
dish and serve immediately.

Macaroni & Corn Pancakes

This vegetable pancake can be filled with your favourite vegetables, as long as they are cooked beforehand. A favourite alternative is shredded parsnips with 1 tbsp mustard.

Serves 4

INGREDIENTS

2 corn cobs
60 g/2 oz/4 tbsp butter
115 g/4 oz red (bell) peppers, cored, seeded and finely diced
285 g/10 oz/2^1/$_2$ cups dried short-cut macaroni

150 ml/1/4 pint/^{5}/$_8$ cup double (heavy) cream
25 g/1 oz/^{1}/$_4$ cup plain (all purpose) flour
4 egg yolks
4 tbsp olive oil

salt and pepper

TO SERVE:
oyster mushrooms
fried leeks

1 Bring a saucepan of water to the boil, add the corn cobs and cook for about 8 minutes. Drain thoroughly and refresh under cold running water for 3 minutes. Carefully cut away the kernels on to kitchen paper (towels) and set aside to dry.

2 Melt 25 g/1 oz/2 tbsp of the butter in a frying pan (skillet). Add the (bell) peppers and cook over a low heat for 4 minutes. Drain and pat dry with kitchen paper (towels).

3 Bring a large saucepan of lightly salted water to the boil. Add the macaroni and cook for about 12 minutes, until tender but still firm to the bite. Drain the macaroni thoroughly and leave to cool in cold water until required.

4 Beat together the cream, flour, a pinch of salt and the egg yolks in a bowl until smooth. Add the corn and (bell) peppers to the cream and egg mixture. Drain the macaroni and then toss into the corn and cream mixture.

Season well with black pepper to taste.

5 Heat the remaining butter with the oil in a large frying pan (skillet). Drop spoonfuls of the mixture into the pan and press down until the mixture forms a flat pancake. Fry until golden on both sides, and all the mixture is used up. Serve immediately with oyster mushrooms and fried leeks.

Vermicelli Flan

*Lightly cooked vermicelli is pressed into a flan ring
and baked with a creamy mushroom filling.*

Serves 4

INGREDIENTS

75 g/3 oz/6 tbsp butter, plus extra,
  for greasing
225 g/8 oz dried vermicelli or
  spaghetti
1 tbsp olive oil
1 onion, chopped

140 g/5 oz button mushrooms
1 green (bell) pepper, cored, seeded
  and sliced into thin rings
150 ml/^{1}/4 pint/^{5}/8 cup milk
3 eggs, lightly beaten
2 tbsp double (heavy) cream

1 tsp dried oregano
freshly grated nutmeg
1 tbsp freshly grated Parmesan
  cheese
salt and pepper
tomato and basil salad, to serve

1 Generously grease a 20 cm/
8 inch loose-based flan tin
(pan) with butter.

2 Bring a large pan of lightly
salted water to the boil. Add
the vermicelli and olive oil and
cook until tender, but still firm to
the bite. Drain, return to the pan,
add 25 g/1 oz/2 tbsp of the butter
and shake the pan to coat the pasta.

3 Press the pasta on to the base
and around the sides of the
flan tin (pan) to make a flan case.

4 Melt the remaining butter in a
frying pan (skillet) over a
medium heat. Add the onion and
fry until it is translucent.

5 Add the mushrooms and
(bell) pepper rings to the
frying pan (skillet) and cook,
stirring, for 2–3 minutes. Spoon
the onion, mushroom and (bell)
pepper mixture into the flan case
and press it evenly into the base.

6 Beat together the milk, eggs
and cream, stir in the oregano

and season to taste with nutmeg
and black pepper. Carefully pour
the mixture over the vegetables
and sprinkle over the cheese.

7 Bake the flan in a preheated
oven at 180°C/350°F/Gas 4
for 40–45 minutes, until the filling
has set.

8 Slide the flan out of the tin
(pan) and serve warm with a
tomato and basil salad.

Fettuccine with Olive, Garlic & Walnut Sauce

This mouth-watering dish would make an excellent light, vegetarian lunch for four or a good starter for six.

Serves 4–6

INGREDIENTS

2 thick slices wholemeal (whole-wheat) bread, crusts removed
300 ml/^{1}/$_2$ pint/1^1/$_4$ cups milk
275/9^1/$_2$ oz/2^1/$_2$ cups shelled walnuts
2 garlic cloves, crushed

115 g/4 oz/1 cup stoned (pitted) black olives
60 g/2 oz/^{2}/$_3$ cup freshly grated Parmesan cheese
8 tbsp extra virgin olive oil

150 ml/^{1}/$_4$ pint/^{5}/$_8$ cup double (heavy) cream
460 g/1 lb fresh fettuccine
salt and pepper
2–3 tbsp chopped fresh parsley

1 Put the bread in a shallow dish, pour over the milk and set aside to soak until the liquid has been absorbed.

2 Spread the walnuts out on a baking (cookie) sheet and toast in a preheated oven at 190°C/375°F/Gas Mark 5 for about 5 minutes, until golden. Set aside to cool.

3 Put the soaked bread, walnuts, garlic, olives, Parmesan cheese and 6 tbsp of the olive oil in a food processor and work to make a purée. Season to taste with salt and black pepper and stir in the cream.

4 Bring a large pan of lightly salted water to the boil. Add the fettuccine and 1 tbsp of the remaining oil and cook for 2–3 minutes, until tender but still firm to the bite. Drain the fettuccine thoroughly and toss with the remaining olive oil.

5 Divide the fettuccine between individual serving plates and spoon the olive, garlic and walnut sauce on top. Sprinkle over the fresh parsley and serve.

COOK'S TIP

Parmesan quickly loses its pungency and 'bite'. It is better to buy small quantities and grate it yourself. Wrapped in foil, it will keep in the refrigerator for several months.

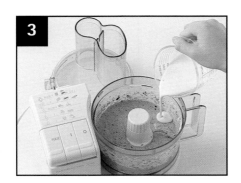

Linguine with Braised Fennel

*This aniseed-flavoured vegetable gives that
extra punch to this delicious creamy pasta dish.*

Serves 4

INGREDIENTS

6 fennel bulbs
150 ml/¹/₄ pint/⁵/₈ cup
   vegetable stock
25 g/1 oz/2 tbsp butter
6 slices rindless smoked bacon, diced

6 shallots, quartered
25 g/1 oz/¹/₄ cup plain (all
   purpose) flour
7 tbsp double (heavy) cream

1 tbsp Madeira
450 g/1 lb dried linguine
1 tbsp olive oil
salt and pepper

1 Trim the fennel bulbs, then gently peel off and reserve the first layer of the bulbs. Cut the bulbs into quarters and put them in a large saucepan, together with the vegetable stock and the reserved outer layers. Bring to the boil, lower the heat and simmer for 5 minutes.

2 Using a slotted spoon, transfer the fennel to a large dish. Discard the outer layers of the fennel bulb. Bring the vegetable stock to the boil and allow to reduce by half. Set aside.

3 Melt the butter in a frying pan (skillet). Add the bacon and shallots and fry for 4 minutes. Add the flour, reduced stock, cream and Madeira and cook, stirring constantly, for 3 minutes, until the sauce is smooth. Season to taste with salt and black pepper and pour over the fennel.

4 Bring a large saucepan of lightly salted water to the boil. Add the linguine and olive oil and cook for 10 minutes, until tender but still firm to the bite. Drain and transfer to a deep ovenproof dish.

5 Add the fennel and sauce and braise in a preheated oven at 180°C/350°F/Gas 4 for 20 minutes. Serve immediately.

COOK'S TIP

Fennel will keep in the salad drawer of the refrigerator for 2–3 days, but it is best eaten as fresh as possible. Cut surfaces turn brown quickly, so do not prepare it too much in advance of cooking.

Baked Aubergines (Eggplant) with Pasta

*Combined with tomatoes and mozzarella cheese, pasta
makes a tasty filling for baked aubergine (eggplant) shells.*

Serves 4

INGREDIENTS

225 g/8 oz dried penne or other short
  pasta shapes
4 tbsp olive oil, plus extra for
  brushing
2 aubergines (eggplant)

1 large onion, chopped
2 garlic cloves, crushed
400 g/14 oz can chopped tomatoes
2 tsp dried oregano
60 g/2 oz mozzarella cheese,
  thinly sliced

25 g/1 oz/^{1}/$_3$ cup freshly grated
  Parmesan cheese
2 tbsp dry breadcrumbs
salt and pepper
salad leaves (greens), to serve

1 Bring a saucepan of lightly salted water to the boil. Add the pasta and 1 tbsp of the olive oil and cook until tender, but still firm to the bite. Drain, return to the pan, cover and keep warm.

2 Cut the aubergines (eggplant) in half lengthways and score around the inside with a sharp knife, being careful not to pierce the shells. Scoop out the flesh with a spoon. Brush the insides of the shells with olive oil. Chop the flesh and set aside.

3 Heat the remaining oil in a frying pan (skillet). Fry the onion until translucent. Add the garlic and fry for 1 minute. Add the chopped aubergine (eggplant) and fry, stirring frequently, for 5 minutes. Add the tomatoes and oregano and season to taste with salt and pepper. Bring to the boil and simmer for 10 minutes, or until thickened. Remove from the heat and stir in the pasta.

4 Brush a baking (cookie) sheet with oil and arrange the aubergine (eggplant) shells in a single layer. Divide half the tomato and pasta mixture between them. Sprinkle over the mozzarella, then pile the remaining tomato and pasta mixture on top. Mix the Parmesan cheese and breadcrumbs and sprinkle over the top, patting it lightly into the mixture.

5 Bake in a preheated oven at 200°C/400°C/Gas 6 for 25 minutes, until the topping is golden brown. Serve hot with salad leaves (greens).

Pasta with Green Vegetable Sauce

The different shapes and textures of the vegetables make a mouth-watering presentation in this light and summery dish.

Serves 4

INGREDIENTS

225 g/8 oz/2 cups dried gemelli or
  other pasta shapes
1 tbsp olive oil
1 head green broccoli, cut into
  florets (flowerets)
2 courgettes (zucchini), sliced

225 g/8 oz asparagus spears
115 g/4 oz mangetout (snow peas)
115 g/4 oz frozen peas
25 g/1 oz/2 tbsp butter
3 tbsp vegetable stock
4 tbsp double (heavy) cream

freshly grated nutmeg
2 tbsp chopped fresh parsley
2 tbsp freshly grated
  Parmesan cheese
salt and pepper

1 Bring a large saucepan of lightly salted water to the boil. Add the pasta and olive oil and cook until tender, but still firm to the bite. Drain, return to the pan, cover and keep warm.

2 Steam the broccoli, courgettes (zucchini), asparagus spears and mangetout (snow peas) over a pan of boiling salted water until they are just beginning to soften. Remove from the heat and refresh in cold water. Drain and set aside.

3 Bring a small pan of lightly salted water to the boil. Add the frozen peas and cook for 3 minutes. Drain the peas, refresh in cold water and then drain again. Set aside with the other vegetables.

4 Put the butter and vegetable stock in a pan over a medium heat. Add all of the vegetables, reserving a few of the asparagus spears, and toss carefully with a wooden spoon until they have heated through, taking care not to break them up.

5 Stir in the cream and heat through without bringing to the boil. Season to taste with salt, pepper and nutmeg.

6 Transfer the pasta to a warmed serving dish and stir in the chopped parsley. Spoon over the vegetable sauce and sprinkle over the Parmesan cheese. Arrange the reserved asparagus spears in a pattern on top and serve.

Niçoise with Pasta Shells

*This is a more filling variation on the traditional
Niçoise salad from southern France.*

Serves 4

INGREDIENTS

350 g/12 oz dried small pasta shells
1 tbsp olive oil
115 g/4 oz green (French) beans
50 g/1³/₄ oz can anchovies, drained
25 m/1 fl oz/¹/₈ cup milk
2 small crisp lettuces

460 g/1 lb or 3 large beef tomatoes
4 hard-boiled (hard-cooked) eggs
225 g/8 oz can tuna, drained
115 g/4 oz/1 cup stoned (pitted)
   black olives
salt and pepper

VINAIGRETTE DRESSING:
50 ml/2 fl oz extra virgin olive oil
25 ml/1 fl oz white wine vinegar
1 tsp wholegrain mustard
salt and pepper

1 Bring a large saucepan of lightly salted water to the boil. Add the pasta and the olive oil and cook until tender, but still firm to the bite. Drain and refresh in cold water.

2 Bring a small saucepan of lightly salted water to the boil. Add the beans and cook for 10–12 minutes, until tender but still firm to the bite. Drain, refresh in cold water, drain thoroughly once more and then set aside.

3 Put the anchovies in a shallow bowl, pour over the milk and set aside for 10 minutes. Meanwhile, tear the lettuces into large pieces. Blanch the tomatoes in boiling water for 1–2 minutes, then drain, skin and roughly chop the flesh. Shell the eggs and cut into quarters. Cut the tuna into large chunks.

4 Drain the anchovies and the pasta. Put all of the salad ingredients, the beans and the olives into a large bowl and gently mix together.

5 To make the vinaigrette dressing, beat together all the dressing ingredients and keep in the refrigerator until required. Just before serving, pour the vinaigrette dressing over the salad.

COOK'S TIP

It is very convenient to make salad dressings in a screw top jar. Put all the ingredients in the jar, cover securely and shake well to mix and emulsify the oil.

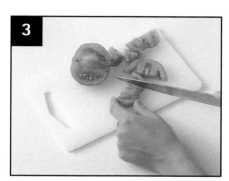

Pasta & Herring Salad

This salad, which so many countries claim as their own,
is also considered in Holland to be a typically Dutch dish.

Serves 4

INGREDIENTS

250 g/9 oz dried pasta shells
5 tbsp olive oil
400 g/14 oz rollmop herrings in brine
6 boiled potatoes
2 large tart apples

2 baby frisée lettuces
2 baby beetroot (beet)
4 hard-boiled (hard-cooked) eggs
6 pickled onions
6 pickled gherkins (dill pickles)

2 tbsp capers
3 tbsp of tarragon vinegar
salt and pepper

1 Bring a large saucepan of lightly salted water to the boil. Add the pasta and 1 tbsp of the olive oil and cook until tender, but still firm to the bite. Drain the pasta thoroughly and then refresh in cold water.

2 Cut the herrings, potatoes, apples, frisée lettuces and beetroot (beet) into small pieces. Put all of these ingredients into a large salad bowl.

3 Drain the pasta thoroughly and add to the salad bowl.

Toss lightly to mix the pasta and herring mixture together.

4 Carefully shell and slice the eggs. Garnish the salad with the slices of egg, pickled onions gherkins (dill pickles) and capers, sprinkle with the remaining olive oil and the tarragon vinegar and serve immediately.

COOK'S TIP

Store this salad, without the dressing, in a container in the refrigerator.

COOK'S TIP

Tarragon vinegar is available from most supermarkets, but you can easily make your own. Add a bunch of fresh tarragon to a bottle of white or red wine vinegar and leave to infuse for 48 hours. It is important to ensure that the tarragon is as fresh as possible and to discard any blemished leaves.

Neapolitan Seafood Salad with Campanelle

This delicious mix of seafood, salad leaves (greens) and ripe tomatoes conjures up all the warmth and sunshine of Naples.

Serves 4

INGREDIENTS

450 g/1 lb prepared squid, cut
  into strips
750 g/1 lb 10 oz cooked mussels
450 g/1 lb cooked cockles in brine
150 ml/$^{1}/_{2}$ pint/$^{5}/_{8}$ cup white wine

300 ml/$^{1}/_{2}$ pint/1$^{1}/_{4}$ cups olive oil
225 g/8 oz/2 cups dried campanelle
  or other small pasta shapes
juice of 1 lemon
1 bunch chives, snipped

1 bunch fresh parsley, finely chopped
4 large tomatoes, quartered or sliced
mixed salad leaves (greens)
salt and pepper
sprig of fresh basil, to garnish

1 Put all of the seafood into a large bowl, pour over the wine and half the olive oil, and set aside for 6 hours.

2 Put the seafood mixture into a saucepan and simmer over a low heat for 10 minutes. Set aside to cool.

3 Bring a large saucepan of lightly salted water to the boil. Add the pasta and 1 tbsp of the remaining olive oil and cook until tender, but still firm to the bite. Drain thoroughly and refresh in cold water.

4 Strain off about half of the cooking liquid from the seafood and discard the rest. Mix in the lemon juice, chives, parsley and the remaining olive oil. Season to taste with salt and pepper. Drain the pasta and add to the seafood.

5 Cut the tomatoes into quarters. Shred the salad leaves (greens) and arrange them at the base of a salad bowl. Spoon in the seafood salad and garnish with the quartered or sliced tomatoes and a sprig of basil.

VARIATION

You can substitute cooked scallops for the mussels and clams in brine for the cockles.

Dolcelatte, Nut & Pasta Salad

*Use colourful salad leaves (greens) to provide visual contrast
to match the contrasts of taste and texture.*

Serves 4

INGREDIENTS

225 g/8 oz/2 cups dried pasta shells
1 tbsp olive oil
115 g/4 oz/1 cup shelled and halved
 walnuts
mixed salad leaves (greens), such
 as radicchio, escarole, rocket

(arugula), lamb's lettuce (corn
salad) and frisée
225 g/8 oz dolcelatte cheese,
 crumbled
salt

DRESSING:
2 tbsp walnut oil
4 tbsp extra virgin olive oil
2 tbsp red wine vinegar
salt and pepper

1 Bring a large saucepan of lightly salted water to the boil. Add the pasta shells and olive oil and cook until just tender, but still firm to the bite. Drain the pasta, refresh under cold running water, drain thoroughly again and set aside.

2 Spread out the shelled walnut halves on to a baking (cookie) sheet and toast under a preheated grill (broiler) for 2–3 minutes. Set aside to cool while you make the dressing.

3 To make the dressing, whisk together the walnut oil, olive oil and vinegar in a small bowl, and season to taste with salt and black pepper.

4 Arrange the salad leaves (greens) in a large serving bowl. Pile the cooled pasta in the middle of the salad leaves (greens) and sprinkle over the dolcelatte cheese. Pour the dressing over the pasta salad, scatter over the walnut halves and toss together to mix. Serve immediately.

COOK'S TIP

Dolcelatte is a semi-soft, blue-veined cheese from Italy. Its texture is creamy and smooth and the flavour is delicate, but piquant. You could substitute Roquefort as an alternative. Whichever cheese you choose, it is essential that it is of the best quality and in peak condition.

Goat's Cheese with Penne, Pear & Walnut Salad

This superb salad was created especially to accompany venison cooked in Chablis, but is equally delicious with other strongly flavoured meat dishes.

Serves 4

INGREDIENTS

260 g/9 oz dried penne
5 tbsp olive oil
1 head radicchio, torn into pieces
1 Webbs lettuce, torn into pieces
7 tbsp chopped walnuts

2 ripe pears, cored and diced
1 fresh basil sprig
1 bunch of watercress, trimmed
2 tbsp lemon juice
3 tbsp garlic vinegar

4 tomatoes, quartered
1 small onion, sliced
1 large carrot, grated
250 g/9 oz goat's cheese, diced
salt and pepper

1 Bring a large saucepan of lightly salted water to the boil. Add the penne and 1 tbsp of the olive oil and cook until tender, but still firm to the bite. Drain the pasta, refresh under cold running water, drain thoroughly again and set aside to cool.

2 Place the radicchio and Webbs lettuce in a large salad bowl and mix together well. Top with the pasta, walnuts, pears, basil and watercress.

3 Mix together the lemon juice, the remaining olive oil and the vinegar in a measuring jug (pitcher). Pour the mixture over the salad ingredients and toss to coat the salad leaves well.

4 Add the tomato quarters, onion slices, grated carrot and diced goat's cheese and toss together, using 2 forks, until well mixed. Leave the salad to chill in the refrigerator for about 1 hour before serving.

COOK'S TIP

Most goat's cheese comes from France and there are many varieties, such as Crottin de Chavignol, Chabi, which is very pungent, and Sainte-Maure, which is available in creamery and farmhouse varieties.

Pasta & Garlic Mayo Salad

This crisp salad would make an excellent accompaniment to grilled (broiled) meat and is ideal for summer barbecues.

Serves 4

INGREDIENTS

2 large lettuces
260 g/9 oz dried penne
1 tbsp olive oil
8 red eating apples

juice of 4 lemons
1 head of celery, sliced
115 g/4 oz/$^3/_4$ cup shelled,
   halved walnuts

250 ml/9 fl oz/1$^1/_8$ cups fresh garlic
   mayonnaise (see Cook's Tip, below
   right)
salt

1 Wash, drain and pat dry the lettuce leaves with kitchen paper. Transfer them to the refrigerator for 1 hour until crisp.

2 Meanwhile, bring a large saucepan of lightly salted water to the boil. Add the pasta and olive oil and cook until tender, but still firm to the bite. Drain the pasta and refresh under cold running water. Drain thoroughly again and set aside.

3 Core and dice the apples, place them in a small bowl and sprinkle with the lemon juice.

Mix together the pasta, celery, apples and walnuts and toss the mixture in the garlic mayonnaise (see Cook's Tip, right). Add more mayonnaise, if liked.

4 Line a salad bowl with the lettuce leaves and spoon the pasta salad into the lined bowl. Serve when required.

COOK'S TIP

Sprinkling the apples with lemon juice will prevent them from turning brown.

COOK'S TIP

To make homemade garlic mayonnaise, beat 2 egg yolks with a pinch of salt and 6 crushed garlic cloves. Start beating in 350 ml/ 12 fl oz/1½ cups olive oil, 1–2 tsp at a time, using a balloon whisk or electric mixer. When about one quarter of the oil has been incorporated, beat in 1–2 tbsp white wine vinegar. Continue beating in the oil, adding it in a thin, continuous stream. Finally, stir in 1 tsp Dijon mustard and season to taste with salt and pepper.

Fusilli, Avocado, Tomato & Mozzarella Salad

Tomatoes and mozzarella cheese are a classic Italian combination.
Here they are joined with pasta spirals and avocado pear for an extra touch of luxury.

Serves 4

INGREDIENTS

2 tbsp pine nuts (kernels)
175 g/6 oz/1^{1}/$_{2}$ cups dried fusilli
1 tbsp olive oil
6 tomatoes
225 g/8 oz mozzarella cheese

1 large avocado pear
2 tbsp lemon juice
3 tbsp chopped fresh basil
salt and pepper
fresh basil sprigs, to garnish

DRESSING:
6 tbsp extra virgin olive oil
2 tbsp white wine vinegar
1 tsp wholegrain mustard
pinch of sugar

1 Spread the pine nuts (kernels) out on a baking (cookie) sheet and toast under a preheated grill (broiler) for 1–2 minutes. Remove and set aside to cool.

2 Bring a large saucepan of lightly salted water to the boil. Add the fusilli and olive oil and cook until tender, but still firm to the bite. Drain the pasta and refresh in cold water. Drain again and set aside to cool.

3 Thinly slice the tomatoes and the mozzarella cheese.

4 Cut the avocado pear in half, remove the stone (pit) and skin. Cut into thin slices lengthways and sprinkle with lemon juice to prevent discoloration.

5 To make the dressing, whisk together the oil, vinegar, mustard and sugar in a small bowl, and season to taste with salt and black pepper.

6 Arrange the tomatoes, mozzarella cheese and avocado pear alternately in overlapping slices on a large serving platter.

7 Toss the pasta with half of the dressing and the chopped basil and season to taste with salt and black pepper. Spoon the pasta into the centre of the platter and pour over the remaining dressing. Sprinkle over the pine nuts (kernels), garnish with fresh basil sprigs and serve immediately.

Pasta-stuffed Tomatoes

*This unusual and inexpensive dish would make a good starter
for eight people or a delicious lunch for four.*

Serves 4

INGREDIENTS

5 tbsp extra virgin olive oil, plus extra
for greasing
8 beef tomatoes or large round
tomatoes

115 g/4 oz/1 cup dried ditalini or
other very small pasta shapes
8 black olives, stoned (pitted) and
finely chopped
2 tbsp finely chopped fresh basil

1 tbsp finely chopped fresh parsley
60 g/2 oz/$^2/_3$ cup freshly grated
Parmesan cheese
salt and pepper
fresh basil sprigs, to garnish

1 Brush a baking (cookie) sheet
with olive oil.

2 Slice the tops off the
tomatoes and reserve to make
'lids'. If the tomatoes will not
stand up, cut a thin slice off the
bottom of each tomato.

3 Using a teaspoon, scoop
out the tomato pulp into a
strainer, but do not pierce the
tomato shells. Invert the tomato
shells on to kitchen paper
(towels), pat dry and then set aside
to drain.

4 Bring a large saucepan of
lightly salted water to the boil.
Add the ditalini or other pasta and
1 tbsp of the remaining olive oil
and cook until tender, but still firm
to the bite. Drain the pasta
thoroughly and set aside.

5 Put the olives, chopped basil,
parsley and Parmesan cheese
into a large mixing bowl and stir in
the drained tomato pulp. Add the
pasta to the bowl. Stir in the
remaining olive oil, mix together
well, and season to taste with salt
and pepper.

6 Spoon the pasta mixture into
the tomato shells and replace
the lids. Arrange the tomatoes on
the baking (cookie) sheet and bake
in a preheated oven at 190°C/
375°F/Gas 5 for 15–20 minutes.

7 Remove the tomatoes from
the oven and allow to cool
until just warm. Arrange on a
serving dish, garnish with the basil
sprigs and serve.

Rare Beef Pasta Salad

This salad is a meal in itself and would be perfect for an al fresco lunch, perhaps with a bottle of red wine.

Serves 4

INGREDIENTS

450 g/1 lb rump or sirloin steak in one piece
450 g/1 lb dried fusilli
5 tbsp olive oil
2 tbsp lime juice

2 tbsp Thai fish sauce (see Cook's Tip, below right)
2 tsp clear honey
4 spring onions (scallions), sliced

1 cucumber, peeled and cut into 2.5 cm/1 inch chunks
3 tomatoes, cut into wedges
3 tsp finely chopped fresh mint
salt and pepper

1 Season the steak with salt and black pepper. Grill (broil) or pan-fry the steak for 4 minutes on each side. Allow to rest for 5 minutes, then slice thinly across the grain.

2 Meanwhile, bring a large saucepan of lightly salted water to the boil. Add the fusilli and 1 tbsp of the olive oil and cook until tender, but still firm to the bite. Drain the fusilli, refresh in cold water and drain again thoroughly. Toss the fusilli in the remaining olive oil.

3 Combine the lime juice, fish sauce and honey in a small saucepan and cook over a medium heat for 2 minutes.

4 Add the spring onions (scallions), cucumber, tomatoes and mint to the pan, then add the steak and mix well. Season to taste with salt.

5 Transfer the fusilli to a large, warm serving dish and top with the steak and salad mixture. Serve just warm or allow to cool completely.

COOK'S TIP

Thai fish sauce, also known as nam pla, is made from salted anchovies and has quite a strong flavour, so it should be used with discretion. It is available from some supermarkets and from Oriental food stores.

Beetroot (Beet) Cannolicchi

Quick and simple, this colourful, warm salad works equally well as a tasty starter or as a main dish.

Serves 4

INGREDIENTS

300 g/11 oz dried ditalini rigati
5 tbsp olive oil
2 garlic cloves, chopped
400 g/14 oz can chopped tomatoes

400 g/14 oz cooked beetroot, diced
2 tbsp chopped fresh basil leaves
1 tsp mustard seeds
salt and pepper

TO SERVE:
mixed salad leaves (greens), tossed in
    olive oil
4 Italian plum tomatoes, sliced

1 Bring a large saucepan of lightly salted water to the boil. Add the pasta and 1 tbsp of the oil and cook for about 10 minutes, until tender, but still firm to the bite. Drain the pasta thoroughly and set aside.

2 Heat the remaining olive oil in a large saucepan. Add the garlic and fry for 3 minutes. Add the chopped tomatoes and cook for 10 minutes.

3 Remove the pan from the heat and carefully add the beetroot (beet), basil, mustard seeds and pasta and season to taste with salt and black pepper.

4 Serve on a bed of mixed salad leaves (greens) tossed in olive oil, and sliced plum tomatoes.

COOK'S TIP

To cook raw beetroot (beet), trim off the leaves about 5 cm/2 inches above the root and ensure that the skin is not broken. Boil in very lightly salted water for 30–40 minutes, until tender. Leave to cool and rub off the skin.

COOK'S TIP

Mustard seeds come from three different plants and may be black, brown or white. Black and brown mustard seeds have a stronger, more pungent flavour than white mustard.

Desserts

If when you think about cooking with pasta, desserts do not usually spring to the forefront of your mind, you will be amazed by the wonderfully self-indulgent sweet treats in this chapter. Who could resist Honey & Walnut Nests, a scrumptious combination of pistachio nuts, honey and crisp angel hair pasta? Raspberry Fusilli is a feast for the eyes as well as the tastebuds, German Noodle Pudding is a rich and satisfying dessert based on a traditional Jewish recipe and Baked Sweet Ravioli is a revelation to anyone with a sweet tooth. The recipes in this chapter will convince you that pasta desserts are much more exciting than a macaroni milk pudding and your family and guests will be delighted with such imaginative ways to end a meal.

Baked Sweet Ravioli

These scrumptious little parcels are the perfect
dessert for anyone with a really sweet tooth.

Serves 4

INGREDIENTS

PASTA:
425 g/15 oz/3³/₄ cups plain
  (all purpose) flour
140 g/ 5 oz/10 tbsp butter, plus extra
  for greasing
140 g/ 5 oz/³/₄ cup caster
  (superfine) sugar

4 eggs
25 g/1 oz yeast
125 ml/4 fl oz warm milk

FILLING:
175 g/6 oz/²/₃ cup chestnut purée
60 g/2 oz/¹/₂ cup cocoa powder

60 g/2 oz/¹/₄ cup caster
  (superfine) sugar
60 g/2 oz/¹/₂ cup chopped almonds
60 g/2 oz/1 cup crushed amaretti
  biscuits (cookies)
175 g/6 oz/⁵/₈ cup
  orange marmalade

1 To make the sweet pasta dough, sift the flour into a mixing bowl, then mix in the butter, sugar and 3 eggs.

2 Mix together the yeast and warm milk in a small bowl and when thoroughly combined, mix into the dough.

3 Knead the dough for 20 minutes, cover with a clean cloth and set aside in a warm place for 1 hour to rise.

4 Mix together the chestnut purée, cocoa powder, sugar, almonds, crushed amaretti biscuits (cookies) and orange marmalade in a separate bowl.

5 Grease a baking (cookie) sheet with butter.

6 Lightly flour the work surface (counter). Roll out the pasta dough into a thin sheet and cut into 5 cm/2 inch rounds with a plain pastry cutter.

7 Put a spoonful of filling on to each round and then fold in half, pressing the edges to seal. Arrange on the prepared baking (cookie) sheet, spacing the ravioli out well.

8 Beat the remaining egg and brush all over the ravioli to glaze. Bake in a preheated oven at 180°C/350°F/Gas 4 for 20 minutes. Serve hot.

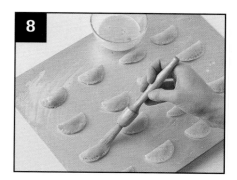

German Noodle Pudding

This rich and satisfying pudding is a traditional Jewish recipe.

Serves 4

INGREDIENTS

60 g/2 oz/4 tbsp butter, plus extra
  for greasing
175 g/6 oz ribbon egg noodles
115 g/4 oz/$^1/_2$ cup cream cheese
225 g/8 oz/1 cup cottage cheese
90 g/3 oz/$^1/_2$ cup caster
  (superfine) sugar

2 eggs, lightly beaten
125 ml/4 fl oz/$^1/_2$ cup soured cream
1 tsp vanilla essence (extract)
a pinch of ground cinnamon
1 tsp grated lemon rind
25 g/1 oz/$^1/_4$ cup flaked
  (slivered) almonds

25 g/1 oz/$^3/_8$ cup dry
  white breadcrumbs
icing (confectioner's) sugar,
  for dusting

1 Grease an ovenproof dish with butter.

2 Bring a large pan of water to the boil. Add the noodles and cook until almost tender. Drain and set aside.

3 Beat together the cream cheese, cottage cheese and caster (superfine) sugar in a mixing bowl. Beat in the eggs, a little at a time. Stir in the soured cream, vanilla essence (extract), cinnamon and lemon rind, and fold in the noodles. Transfer the mixture to the prepared dish and smooth the surface.

4 Melt the butter in a frying pan (skillet). Add the almonds and fry, stirring constantly, for about 1–1½ minutes, until lightly coloured. Remove the frying pan (skillet) from the heat and stir the breadcrumbs into the almonds.

5 Sprinkle the almond and breadcrumb mixture over the pudding and bake in a preheated oven at 180°C/350°F/Gas 4 for 35-40 minutes, until just set. Dust with a little icing (confectioner's) sugar and serve immediately.

VARIATION

Although not authentic, you could add 3 tbsp raisins with the lemon rind in step 3, if liked.

Honey & Walnut Nests

*Pistachio nuts and honey are combined with crisp cooked
angel hair pasta in this unusual Greek dessert.*

Serves 4

INGREDIENTS

225 g/8 oz angel hair pasta
115 g/4 oz/8 tbsp butter
175 g/6 oz/1^1/$_2$ cups shelled
  pistachio nuts, chopped

115 g/4 oz/^{1}/$_2$ cup sugar
115 g/4 oz/^{1}/$_3$ cup clear honey
150 ml/^{1}/$_4$ pint/^{5}/$_8$ cup water
2 tsp lemon juice

salt
Greek-style yogurt, to serve

1 Bring a large saucepan of
lightly salted water to the
boil. Add the angel hair pasta and
cook until tender, but still firm to
the bite. Drain the pasta and
return to the pan. Add the butter
and toss to coat the pasta
thoroughly. Set aside to cool.

2 Arrange 4 small flan or
poaching rings on a baking
(cookie) sheet. Divide the angel
hair pasta into 8 equal quantities
and spoon 4 of them into the
rings. Press down lightly. Top the
pasta with half of the nuts, then
add the remaining pasta.

3 Bake in a preheated oven at
180°C/350°F/Gas 4 for
45 minutes, until golden brown.

4 Meanwhile, put the sugar,
honey and water in a
saucepan and bring to the boil over
a low heat, stirring constantly until
the sugar has dissolved completely.
Simmer for 10 minutes, add the
lemon juice and simmer for a
further 5 minutes.

5 Using a palette knife
(spatula), carefully transfer
the angel hair nests to a serving
dish. Pour over the honey syrup,

sprinkle over the remaining nuts
and set aside to cool completely
before serving. Hand the Greek-
style yogurt separately.

COOK'S TIP

*Angel hair pasta is also
known as* capelli
d'Angelo. *Long and
very fine, it is usually sold in small
bunches that already resemble nests.*